# Mo
# Conqueror:

Volume 1

*Compiled By:*

*Dr. John E. Gray*

*&*

*Dr. Angie Gray*

Onyx Expressions Publishing

New Jersey

DR. JOHN E. GRAY



SPEAKER COACH
Angie Gray
EMPOWERMENT MATTERS
CONSULTANT AUTHOR



**ISBN: 978-1-959061-00-7**

# What People Are Saying About *More Than a Conqueror*

An EXTREMELY important read! This book is about conquering and overcoming issues associated with mental wellness a common issue of today. It covers all aspects of mental health in all its forms including in some cases physical symptoms. The compilation of stories and testimonies, from Breaking Free from Burnout to For Such a Time As This, underline the fact that mental wellness is not a respecter of persons. This book shows the true resilience of the human spirit and the power of God through unseen angels.

I also took away from this book that everyone has a story. Everyone. Each person's story can be a lifeline to someone else going through a difficult season. We can use our stories to provide hope, tools and understanding.

Everyone should read this book. It's not just for those who are in the middle of the struggle or who are finding themselves feeling the weight of pushing themselves too hard or having to find a way all on their own as a 13 yr. old child, but it's for anyone who knows someone who may have been in one of those places. This book gives an open window into understanding the pain, fear, frustration etc. that accompanies the battle of becoming an overcomer. When you are looking from the outside in, those are easily misunderstood or overlooked. *More Than a Conqueror* gives the full picture. Highly recommend it. I don't think there is anyone who wouldn't benefit greatly from reading this book.

**Review by Charisse Burton, Author, Speaker, Business Strategy & Messaging Coach**

If you have ever endeavored to be the best version of yourself but did not know where to start, then *More Than a Conqueror* is the book for you. We all have times of doubt, have been hurt, felt grief, and suffered setbacks in this life. The authors of this book share their stories to inspire the reader to overcome these challenges to become our best selves. I highly recommend this book!

**Review by Linda McVey**

# DEDICATION

This compilation of stories is dedicated to the Author and Finisher of our faith and to every reader who has within their heart a desire to become better and is willing to make the necessary changes, do the hard work, and keep persevering until they sufficiently glorify His holy name.

# Disclaimer

Please be advised that the information in this book is not meant to replace the advice of a certified professional. The content of this book is for informational purposes only and makes no guarantees concerning the level of success you may experience by following the advice or strategies offered. Please consult a licensed advisor in matters relating to your personal and professional well-being including your mental, emotional and physical health, finances, business, legal matters, family planning, education, and spiritual practices. The views and opinions expressed throughout this book are those of the individual author and do not necessarily reflect the views or opinions of all of the authors or any other agency, organization, employer, publisher, or company.

Also, please note that the views or vision of each of the authors are always subject to change at any time. Please do not hold them or the publisher to them in perpetuity. Any references to previous performances may not be indicative of future results. No warranties or guarantees are expressed or implied by the publisher's choice to include any of the collaborating authors in this volume.

If you choose to attempt any of the methods mentioned in this book, the authors and publisher advise you to take full responsibility for your safety and well-being. The author and

# Table of Contents

Drs. John and Angie Gray
Visionary Authors

# THE MAKING OF CONQUERORS!

**By Dr. John E. Gray & Dr. Angie Gray**
**Visionary Authors**

### ~ About the Vision ~

For those who are familiar with the bible, you will notice that the title of this book is a clear connection to the scripture in the book of Romans, Chapter 8 and Verse 37. In that chapter, Paul is naming a litany of trials and sufferings that God's people endure. He ended the list with a comment of optimism and hope that still rings true. "*We are more than conquerors through Him who love us.*" It was with that connection to the hope and inspiration of that verse that this collaboration came to life.

During the Pandemic and shutdown of 2020 (and beyond), the Drs. Gray discovered that much of the work they were doing with their individual clients was very similar to that which the other was doing. They were each working to empower their clients to become the best version of themselves. While watching *Shark Tank* on tv one evening and seeing two "*sharks*" come together to work with a single entrepreneur, Dr. John and Dr. Angie were inspired to combine their collective skills, resources, and experiences to build a more cohesive effort for their clients.

*~ Visionary Authors: Drs. John & Angie Gray ~*

As they have always supported each other in their individual efforts, it became apparent that it made better sense to unify and create a collaborative experience for their clients. Dr. John's Onyx Expressions and Dr. Angie's Empowerment Center seemed to be a marriage made in heaven. From that union, Empowerment Matters, LLC was born.

During Christmas week of 2021, Dr. Angie fell deathly ill and faced a near-death experience; spending over two weeks in the hospital Intensive Care Unit. She emerged with a message from the Creator. She was divinely inspired to provide the vehicle for others to share their stories of triumph and resilience. She shared this with her husband and together they acknowledged they had mutual experiences that demonstrated the grace, mercy, and favor necessary to become *more than conquerors* and had been called for *such a time as this.* Realizing that there were many who faced and overcame challenges, adversity, and obstacles, they set out to create a space and opportunity for others to share their experiences of tests and testimonies.

*~ Visionary Authors: Drs. John & Angie Gray ~*

# Good Luck With the Rest of Your Life

## Dr. John E. Gray

## Co-Visionary Author

*~ Visionary Author: Dr. John E. Gray ~*

# Good Luck With the Rest of Your Life

**By Dr. John E. Gray**

A few years ago, I began to take inventory of my life's journey, and I can honestly say that I have had several "more than a conqueror" moments. I always say that life will not treat you fairly simply because you have goals and good intentions. There will be times when we must fight in order to survive and thrive.

I am a huge proponent of inspiration. I believe in my soul that there is nothing more powerful than an inspired and determined person. Such people can change the world! We have the ability to draw inspiration from powerful stories of perseverance, resilience, and grit. That is why this book is so important. These pages contain perspectives of hope and endurance that are truly inspirational. It takes a special kind of boldness and courage to put your most vulnerable moments in the pages of a book for the world to see. Each of the authors in this book has made the commitment to inspire the world through the lens of their challenges and moments of doubt, hurt, pain, grief, and suffering.

The one thing we all have in common as humans is that we will each experience moments that don't feel good when they're happening. These things are often weapons that have formed against us and are meant for our harm. Difficulty, challenges, trials, obstacles, and circumstances frequently confront us as we journey through life. It is not a matter of *if* we will experience these things, but it is simply a matter of *when* we do. The *if* and the *when* are not nearly as important as *how* we respond to them. How one chooses to deal with the hand that's been dealt to them will determine the path their life will take. What separates the victor from the defeated is how they confront adversity. Do they fight it or do they simply allow it to happen? The question really comes down to; Do they allow life to happen *to* them or do they make life happen *for* them?

I have dealt with many of life's blows. I lost my mother to breast cancer at the age of 7. The next series of events would certainly change my life forever. I was placed in foster care. When I tried to connect with my father, he abandoned me. I mistakenly thought he was the Calvary coming for me. One night I called him and asked him I could come live him. Much to my relief, he said I could. I packed my bags and caught a bus to Newark, NJ. When I got to the bus station, my dad was nowhere to be found. When I called him to find out where he was, I heard these devastating words, "I don't know why you are waiting for me; I can't do nothing for you." I was left standing in the bus station alone nothing but the two trash bags of clothes I had brought with me.

I lived in a shelter in high school and went to three different high schools in my junior year due to the problems I was facing. I literally fought my way through school. As the angry boy with no parental support to speak of, who lived in a shelter, somebody was always pushing my buttons and trying me. I could never get established anywhere before I had to move again. Somehow, by the grace of God, I graduated from high school and went to college. Unfortunately, my problems didn't end there.

I was literally homeless in college. I can remember standing around waiting for my friends to steal some food from the cafeteria just so I could have something to eat. I didn't have a meal plan and frequently dined on ramen noodles for breakfast, lunch, and dinner. I'm not complaining though, because had I not gone to college, I would never have become the educated man I am today.

My challenges didn't stop upon graduation from college. I have dealt with divorce and loss. I've struggled with the burden of "paycheck to paycheck" finances. I could go on and on, but it really is no need. I say that because this journey really isn't about me, it's about how my experiences can help others. People so often look at the finished product and think the person they say must've always had it together. In many cases, and mine for sure, nothing is further from the truth. I come from very humble beginnings. These are but a few of the things I had to face and fight through. The difference is that I had a champion mentality. I have always been a fighter and simply cannot just allow life to beat up on me while I do nothing. Many people know me today as "Dr. Gray" but do not realize the number of life's landmines I had to navigate through.

One of the most pivotal moments in my life coincides with the title of this chapter. Let me walk you through. As I mentioned previously, I was in foster care and was what was called at that time "a ward of the court". I would wear that status until I aged out of the system on my 18th birthday. Once a ward of the court turned 18 that would be the end of the state's financial obligations. Plainly put, you were on your own! No resources, no assistance, no guidance. Let me share with you my "age out of the system" moment.

I was due to turn 18 on October 31, 1986. At the time, I was a freshman at Stockton State College, which today is Stockton University. I called my caseworker a week before my birthday to arrange the pickup of my last check. My caseworker was located in Newark, which is where I lived, yet I was in southern NJ which is about 2 hours away. When I got her on the phone she confirmed that I had one final check coming to me in the amount of $332. She then told me that the check would be waiting for me when I got there. I explained to her that I was unable to make it up there because I was 2 hours away and had no money for transportation. Her entire demeanor changed because she now had the responsibility of bringing the check to me, as I was still considered a ward of the court on her caseload. She agreed to bring the check, then hung up the phone abruptly. A week later, on my birthday, she agreed to meet in upper J Wing at Stockton. As I sat there waiting for her, it began to dawn on me that I would literally be on my own. While I was under the State's care, at least I had some financial assistance and medical insurance, but it dawned on me that I would not have any such support. I began to think about how I was going to make it with nothing. I didn't have a plan or even a clue, but I knew I had to figure it out.

As I pondered my new reality, I saw my caseworker walking towards me. In my mind, I thought we were going to have a conversation about possible resources, assistance, or anything that could help me as I transitioned out of the system. I soon discovered that there would be no such conversation. I could tell from the moment I could see her face that she was not a happy camper! I already knew that she did not want to make the drive to Stockton to deliver the check, but her face told the whole story. Mind you, this is the person who facilitated my transitions to shelters and foster homes, and I can honestly say that she was very helpful during those times. This is why I was so confused about her demeanor. Here I was, in college, trying to better myself, and I was getting this cold shoulder treatment. What she did after she reached me confirmed the look on her face. She handed me the check, said "Good luck with the rest of your life," and turned around and walked away! What???

Huhhh??? Did she just say, "Good luck with the rest of your life." and turn and walk away?!?!?

I sat there, stunned. All I could think about was how cold and callous that was. I felt that overwhelming feeling of abandonment all over again. The loss of my mother. Being left at the bus station by my father at 13 years old. Getting dropped off at the boys shelter in the middle of the night. I couldn't get those words out of my head…"Good luck with the rest of your life." All I had to my name was that check for $332. I had no idea how I was going to make it, and I am sure the people walking by me as I sat there crying were wondering what was wrong with me. What I did next became my life's mantra. I got up, wiped the tears from my face, and said to myself, *"John Gray, are you going to sink or swim?" I stood there for a second or two and then I said, "You are going to swim."*

I stared down that moment of hardship and adversity with a determination that has served me well. Needless to say, I eventually graduated from Stockton, and I went on to get both a Masters and Doctorate degree. But that is not the totality of the story. Conquering our fears, worries, and anxieties has generational implications. You see, I grew up in poverty and in so much uncertainty. I scraped by to get through college. I had to face down that moment in upper J Wing with resilience and grit. I had to conquer that moment! Here is why it is so important. My life was rocked on my 18th birthday in upper J

Wing, but my redemption was also found at the same location 30 years later! I was able to return to Stockton as the Assistant Dean of the School of Education, and my office was located in, you guessed it, upper J Wing! Every day I walked past the very spot where my spirit was broken. I could smile and feel good, knowing that I had conquered that moment in my life. But I am so thankful that my 18-year-old self decided to fight!

But it gets even better! Because I am now employed at Stockton, it gives me the blessed opportunity to send my children to college TUITION FREE! I went from homeless in higher ed to giving my children the gift of a free college experience! This does not happen if I decided I was not going to swim, and simply gave up because the odds were stacked up against me. Life hands us the lemons, but lemonade sure tastes good! No matter what you face, you have the capacity to endure, survive, and thrive! It begins with the locked-in mindset that you will not be conquered by the adversities you encounter. The best advice I can give you is this: *Get up, wipe the tears from your face, decide to swim, and good luck with the rest of your life!* You are more than a conqueror!!

*~ Visionary Author: Dr. John E. Gray ~*

*Dr. John E. Gray*

Co-Visionary Author

# *About John*

Dr. John Gray is a Purpose and Resilience Coach who works with people of all ages to empower them to use their God-given purpose, gifts and talents to become the best version of themselves so they can leave a lasting legacy for the Universe.

John strongly believes that we each have a divine purpose in life and that we are much happier and productive when we are walking in that purpose. He is of the strong conviction that when individuals lead a purpose-driven life, the Kingdom is a much better place for everyone.

Dr. Gray is an accomplished public speaker and protégé of internationally-renowned motivational speaker, Les Brown. He is also the host of a weekly talk show, ***"PowerTalk."***

Dr. Gray is the Senior Pastor of the Empowered Life Ministries Church in New Jersey. He is also faculty at Stockton University in Galloway, NJ, where he teaches in the *Ed.D in Organizational Leadership* program.

*~ Visionary Author: Dr. John E. Gray ~*

Breaking Free
From Burnout
Jodie Solberg

# Breaking Free From Burnout

**By Jodie Solberg**

At first glance, burnout seemed to arrive without warning. As if there were no signs, no precursors, no symptoms. It was simply there, where yesterday it didn't exist. But upon closer examination, it had been building for years just under the surface, waiting for the most impactful time to strike. This is the story of how chronic burnout reared its monstrous head in my life, how I overcame it, and how you can do the same.

Looking back now, I can see that my burnout journey started when I was young. I was a high achiever, active in multiple sports year-round and, as soon as I was able, began working. Juggling it all was normal to me. Then in high school, my parents got divorced, I moved across the country, and my mother was diagnosed with cancer. I had a lot on my plate, but I pushed through and kept up my grades so I could get into college to become a therapist. Independence was important to me, and I moved away to college just 3 days after graduation, earning 2 degrees in 4 years by going to school year-round, doing 2 internships working with families in crisis and working nights and weekends to help pay my way through school. I took one week off each year at Christmas, making the 24-hour drive straight through to spending a few days visiting family, and then driving back. This grueling pace continued into graduate school for Clinical Psychology. Just before school began, I started a business to help pay off my student loans, and I also met the man who would become my husband. Our relationship was long-distance, and we had opposite schedules, so between spending 60 hours in classes and clinical hours and my homework each week, I wasn't getting adequate sleep. Then 9/11 happened and working in a mental health clinic, I saw the effects of the grief, fear, and the trauma it caused for so many, firsthand. Through that experience, I realized that I had been out of alignment with my values and was headed toward burnout. The constant stress and lack of sleep took their toll on me, and I realized I needed to shift my priorities and change my habits.

Several years after I first experienced symptoms of burnout, it crept back up again. I enjoyed my work, but I was spreading myself too thin. I was often sick and couldn't seem to shake it. I didn't initially recognize it as burnout, I just pushed through and attributed it to working with children. I would tell myself that everyone I worked with got sick, too. Then, I caught a cold that turned into a sinus infection, and an allergic reaction to the antibiotics led to intestinal ulcers. After surgery, I felt pressure to go back to work too soon. My body didn't have time to heal properly, and ultimately the doctors said there was nothing they could do, so I made the decision to take time off to focus on my business and take care of my mother after her own surgery. During that time, I explored what I needed to recover and found a holistic practitioner who helped me to heal my gut and boost my immune system.

After healing, I was healthy for a decade, until the pull of overachieving struck again. I overloaded my plate, and the 60-80-hour weeks and unsustainable case load caught up with me. I was at the pinnacle of success in my career, but it left me fatigued, tied to my phone, and eating out every meal. Then one day, I got hit by a truck - literally. I was stopped in heavy traffic when I heard a crash. When I looked into my rear-view mirror, I saw a big commercial truck hit the vehicle behind me, and seconds later, they pushed through my car and kept going, ending up flipped backward two lanes away. Nearly a year of multiple physical therapy and doctor's visits per week later, I was in constant pain and my body was still not recovering. I was unable to do basic tasks such as carry a purse, or push a shopping cart, let alone work. And on top of everything, my mom was having more health challenges and precious family members passed away. I was at my breaking point and there was no denying it this time. I was completely burned out. That excruciatingly painful year forced me to make some much needed changes. I took time to reflect and ultimately made a complete lifestyle shift. My husband of 20 years and I decided to close our offices down and move away from the city, redesigning our lives to align with our values. I took everything I loved most over my 20 years in both my therapeutic career and my coaching business and built my new private practice around them. Working virtually with clients opened the possibilities of who I could help and gave me the flexibility I needed.

When the pandemic began, it reinforced the fact that I had made the right decision. I examined what led to my burnout, the habits that needed to be replaced, and acknowledged how my independence was a double-edged sword. One of the most important lessons I learned through burnout is that being independent doesn't mean doing everything on my own all the time. I see now that my inner strength is enhanced by surrounding myself with others who lift me up and support me. Having now broken free from chronic burnout, it's vital to continue to be aware of the signs and symptoms so that I can prevent it in the future. Burnout often starts with small signs that are easily brushed off, but when ignored, they grow larger until they are undeniable. It's a continuous cycle and the symptoms can be mental, emotional, and/or physical. There has been knowledge of the mind-body-spirit connection for thousands of years. Burnout is even discussed in the Bible, where rest is encouraged and recognized as necessary. ***Proverbs 17:22*** states that, "A cheerful heart is good medicine, but a crushed spirit dries up the bones." This connection is becoming even more widely recognized since the pandemic began. When I began my therapeutic career, preventative mental wellness wasn't talked about in the media, or even recognized by many doctors outside of the field of psychology. Conversations about mental health automatically meant mental illness. Fortunately, it is now becoming the norm to be more open about mental health, to share our challenges and realize that we are not alone.

Burnout is a term that has only been around since the 1970s, but now it is so prevalent in our society that it is commonly talked about. But what is burnout exactly? Burnout is what happens when you go through an extended period of stress, which causes mental and physical collapse. It includes physical symptoms such as sleep issues, frequent illness, and fatigue. Burnout can also cause mental and emotional challenges, such as depression, anxiety, loss of focus and productivity, irritability, apathy, and memory deficits. With such a wide array of symptoms, burnout begins before you even realize it's happening. Perhaps you take on a new and exciting project for work. At first, you are excited, committed, and full of energy. You're focused and productive. But even things in our lives that are positive can be stressful, especially if we are pushing ourselves by depleting our energy. You may be sleeping less to fit it all in and become a little irritable with people at home. But you ignore it and keep going, saying you'll catch up on sleep later. Over time, the frustration builds, and the fatigue worsens. You're unable to focus, you become anxious and overwhelmed, and you start losing your motivation. Your relationships begin to suffer. You are struggling, but you may be in denial or oblivious about why. You become sick more often, experiencing headaches, chronic pain, or digestive issues. But like I did, you tell yourself it's normal. Until you crash under mental and physical exhaustion and are completely overwhelmed. Left unchecked, this cycle can keep repeating, causing chronic burnout where you never fully recover, you only get well enough to start the process all over again.

If this sounds familiar to you, you're not alone. Burnout rates peaked at their all-time highest levels after the pandemic began in 2020. The average person today experiences more stress in one month than our ancestors had in their entire lifetime. Many people live in a mild state of burnout, which is why it's important to recognize the signs. In our society, it's encouraged and rewarded to work hard and be constantly busy. Having idle time or caring for yourself is labeled as lazy or selfish. In actuality, taking care of yourself is the opposite of those negative labels. When you work long hours without breaks, pile too much onto your plate, and don't set boundaries around your time and energy, it directly contributes to your likelihood of experiencing burnout. Developing good habits and building coping strategies into your daily routine is key. The result is that you will have renewed energy, sustainable overall health, and more fulfillment in all areas of your life.

A common answer to this problem has been work-life balance. But balance often creates even more pressure, trying to keep all the areas of your life perfectly even. That is why I believe instead in creating work-life harmony, taking all the areas of your life, and arranging them in a way that is pleasing for you. At any given time, one area may be the focus, as in the guitar or vocal solo of a song, but overall, the pieces flow together. Doing this can reduce anxiety, stress, and overwhelm, while increasing your self-confidence, self-esteem, inner peace, and happiness. Harmony allows you to have the mental and physical energy to care for others as your best self, giving them the overflow of your energy instead of the leftovers.

There are strategies that I have used myself, and teach my clients, to successfully recover from and prevent burnout. The first is practicing mindfulness to increase your self-awareness. Take a few moments each day to be still, take some deep breaths, and check in with yourself to see how you feel both mentally and physically, and determine what you need in that moment. Practice self-compassion, being kind to yourself as you would to others. The road to health is a lifelong journey, and each of us has an individual path. Focus on the progress you are making on that path, rather than trying to attain an impossible level of perfection.

Next, guard your energy by building regular breaks into your schedule. I no longer rush between appointments, causing myself unnecessary stress. I include breaks between each item on my calendar to give myself time to recharge my energy and do a mental and physical reset, so I have the strength and stamina to give others my best support. Know your limits for how long you can focus before needing a break and when you work best. Turn off notifications that flood your brain with constant information, focusing on one task at a time. Also, learn how you recharge best. What brings you peace and joy? In the height of burnout, I had a very difficult time answering that question, so I had to look deep to find the answer. Swimming, dancing, walks in nature, listening to music, reading, and quiet alone time are some of mine. Find what works for you, and set aside time just for yourself, doing literally anything that you enjoy and find relaxing.

Another strategy is to make a list of your top 10 influences, which could be in- person or virtual, and include the people, books, podcasts, television, and social media you spend time with. They are influencing your thoughts, emotions, and behaviors, and could be contributing to burnout. Write a plus, minus, or equal sign next to each one, based on your self-confidence and energy level after spending time with them. Make a conscious choice to focus your time on the positives, set clear boundaries, and limit interactions with the negatives. Also, periodically re-prioritize your values. Examine the people, things, activities, and ideals that are most important to you. At the top of the list is always your own personal well-being, because without it you cannot be your best self. Once you've put your values in order, look at the decisions you have been making. How are you treating those at the top of your list, and what needs to change for you to be in alignment with your values? Make decisions on and base your goals and your lifestyle on your top values. When you truly know what's important, you can be intentional about your daily activities and make sure they are getting you closer to your goals and fulfilling your purpose.

Practicing mindfulness and gratitude is another way to beat burnout. Release what you can't control and take the time each day for reflection, meditation, prayer, and gratitude. Develop the habit of being appreciative of all the good things in your life. To incorporate this into your daily life, you could start by writing what you are looking forward to each morning, and what went well each evening. Add in something or someone you are grateful for, and why. Gratitude literally changes our brain and improves our overall health and helps us remember that we are not alone. The mistaken belief that you must be all things to all people, all the time leads to burnout. In doing so, we become last on our list and sacrifice our own well-being. When building a sustainable lifestyle, it's not enough just to focus on one aspect of our lives. Dr. Charles F. Glassman stated that, "Stress can destroy much more than our physical health. Too often, it eats away at our hope, faith and belief." Get the support you need to nurture all aspects of your mind, body, and spirit, to break the cycle of burnout in your own life. I have designed my work and life around taking care of myself holistically and teach my clients to do the same. In your own journey, reaching out for support can help you gain the clarity and confidence to take the necessary action to create the life you deserve.

I do not believe people are broken. The trials we go through and the lessons we learn along the way shape us. We become more than conquerors as we overcome our obstacles and heal from our hurts, and we come out of the fire even stronger than before. It's time to take your first step to recovering from and preventing burnout. Make the decision today and then take action to create the lifestyle you dream of. You are capable of and deserve for those dreams to become a reality. Not only can you break free from burnout, but you can be overwhelmingly victorious in creating a life that you love!

# *Jodie Solberg*

Contributing Author

# About Jodie

Jodie Solberg is a Mental Wellness and Success Coach, Certified Master Hypnotherapist, and an International Best-Selling Author. Jodie loves working with purpose-driven professional women on a mission to live in alignment with their passion and values to create real and lasting change in their lives and the world around them. She helps them tap into the power of their subconscious mind to gain the clarity and confidence they need to up-level and achieve both their personal and professional goals.

Jodie has been working therapeutically for more than 20 years, with degrees in both Psychology and Sociology. She started her entrepreneurial journey as a consultant and coach for female entrepreneurs while still in graduate school studying Clinical Psychology, which is where she first began practicing as a Hypnotherapist as well. Jodie's experience working with diverse populations such as women and children suffering from the effects of abuse, teens in after-school programs and group homes, parents in training programs, people dealing with chronic illnesses and addiction, and burned-out caregivers gives her a unique perspective to help her clients overcome their limiting beliefs, break through blocks to progress, and heal past hurts so they can be free from anxiety and fear, beat burnout, and have more peace, joy, and harmony in their personal and professional lives.

Alongside her therapeutic career, Jodie is known for her work as a consultant and a coach for women in business. Her transformative coaching programs build self-esteem and confidence and increase her clients' focus, strength, resilience, and emotional intelligence. She also teaches about the importance of prioritizing self-care so they can go out and give back to their families and communities to create positive changes in the world and serve others as their best selves.

Jodie founded Psyched Up Success in 2019, fulfilling her long-standing dream of having her own private mental wellness practice working virtually with clients worldwide. Jodie's greatest joy and purpose is in helping other women to find their voice, become their best selves, create a life they love, and pass those lessons on to the next generation of strong, independent women. In addition to her professional fulfillment, she is a great contributor to her community with a long history of volunteerism. Jodie has always been a believer in creating work-life harmony, so she enjoys spending time outdoors and traveling with her family in search of great food, music, and culture.

To connect with Jodie, please email her directly at jodie@psychedupsuccess.com or visit her website at www.psychedupsuccess.com. You may also follow her on social media on Instagram at @psyched_up_success or Facebook at @psychedupsuccess

# Better Days Are Coming:

# Joy Comes in the Morning

**Sonya LaVonka**

**Howell Barrow**

# Better Days Are Coming: Joy Comes in the Morning

**By Sonya Howell Barrow**

*"The LORD himself goes before you and will be with you; he will never leave you nor forsake you. Do not be afraid; do not be discouraged." ~ Deuteronomy 31:8*

As I stared at the reflection in the mirror, a scared little African American girl cautiously stared back at me. Her eyes were glossy and filled with tears. Nervously, her lips quivered and trembled in fear. Though frightened, the little girl continued to stare at me in bewilderment. The problem was that I was not the little girl I was looking at in the mirror. We both realized that we were looking at someone different from ourselves. Neither she nor I understood what was going on. She did not understand her reflection in the mirror, and I did not understand mine. The little girl was confused because when she looked at herself, she saw that she was dressed in raggedy clothes, but when she looked in the mirror, she saw something completely different.

In fact, the reflection in the mirror was not of even of a little girl at all. Instead, her reflection was of an adult African American woman outfitted in a United States Army military dress uniform. The front of the formal jacket of the dress uniform was filled with medals, ribbons, and other decorations. Atop of the shoulders of the uniform jacket represented the most important item displayed on the entire uniform, two shiny silver bars with a single black stripe down the middle of each. Those bars represented a significant military accomplishment. The woman in the mirror had achieved the rank of Chief Warrant Officer Five, the highest warrant officer rank within the United States Army.

The little girl continued to look in the mirror and so did the woman, each of them seeing a stranger in the mirror. It was like the magic mirrors at *Ripley's Believe It Or Not.* Continuing to look into the mirror, the little girl and the woman finally realized that they were not strangers at all. The scared little girl dressed in raggedy clothes and the woman dressed in the United States Army dress uniform were one and the same. Both of them were versions of myself; one of who I used to be and one of who I am today. I was looking at the reflection of the girl I used to be and I wondered how did I get to be the woman I am today. Yes, we were one and the same, but we needed to see the separate version of each other. As the little girl, I needed to look ahead and dream about who I could become. Yet, as the woman I had become, I had to look back and see all that I had endured as that little girl in order to find the strength necessary to become the woman I am today and the woman I will become tomorrow.

~ *Sonya LaVonka Howell Barrow* ~

As the woman I had become smiled at the girl I used to be, memories of my life's struggles flashed before my eyes. The little girl I was hesitantly returned the smile and slowly, her once cloudy and teary eyes brightened and dried. They sparkled like a ray of sunshine. With a slight nod of her head, the little girl finally understood her reflection in the mirror. She said, "I get it now. I am looking into my future. The grown woman that I see is who I have become. I am no longer a scared little girl, discarded and disregarded by many. Now I was a grown woman, determined, independent, and unstoppable." Looking at this future version of herself, the little girl transformed into a grown woman - the woman who I am today. It was at that moment that the little girl realized that "better days would come."

*Better days are coming* is what my inner voice told me for many years. Along with God's Grace, despite many obstacles, I consistently excelled throughout my life and my military career. Better days did, in fact, come. As a *Chief Warrant Officer Five*, I am often referred to as a "*Unicorn*." This is simply because the distinction of *Chief Warrant Officer Five* is a status rarely achieved by females, much less African American females. I am grateful, proud, and humbled to have achieved such an exceptional milestone. However, my road to success was far from easy.

*~ Sonya LaVonka Howell Barrow ~*

## Surviving Childhood and Teenage Parenthood

More often than not, there were whispers about the baby with a baby. My mother became pregnant with me at a very young age. Despite the objections of my paternal grandfather, I was born out of wedlock. Rejected by my biological father and grandfather, I was raised by my grandmother and mother. I am the only daughter and the eldest child of three children born to my biological mother. I spent most of my early childhood years mainly with my grandmother. However, during my teenage years, I lived solely with my mother. By the time that I was in high school, my mother was severely addicted to stimulant drugs. Because of her drug addiction, she, my little brother, and I experienced a vicious cycle of poverty and homelessness.

Though still addicted to drugs, homeless, and living in cheap motels, by my junior year of high school, my mother had given birth to her third child, a son. During the summer prior to my senior year in high school, we had moved to an apartment. Shortly thereafter, I found myself in a relationship with a local drug distributor and became pregnant. Meanwhile, my mother continued her drug addictive behavior, which led to us getting evicted from the apartment. We remained homeless until two months prior to the birth of my oldest son. One month after I gave birth, his biological father was sent to prison.

*~ Sonya LaVonka Howell Barrow ~*

Several months later, my son and I moved into an apartment located within a low-income housing development. We lived in that apartment for two and one-half years. While living there, I was unemployed and received Aid to Families with Dependent Children (AFDC – commonly known as Welfare) and supplemental assistance from the Women-Infant-Children (WIC) Program from the State of Georgia. Prior to my 21st birthday, due to my financial circumstances, I decided to give temporary custody of my son to my grandmother in order for me to join the United States Army. This decision would change the entire trajectory of my life - in many ways.

## Surviving the United States Army and Military Deployments, Marriage and Personal and Professional Education

Though I was a frightened young mother, at the age of 20, I joined the United States Army. This was a decision that I made in order to seek a better lifestyle for myself and my son. As a single parent, I was the backbone of my small family. Therefore, I continuously sought ways to improve my personal and professional growth and development. However, in the meantime, I made very poor choices in my relationships. From my conception to birth, I had been rejected by the two most important men in my life. Therefore, I have never known or clearly understood the meaning of love or experienced being truly loved by a man. I believe this, alone, is the number one reason why I have consistently become involved with the wrong type of men. By type of men, I mean that the ones I've connected with have simply used, abused or mistreated me. Between that and realizing I needed a father figure for my oldest son, by the time I met the man that I would later marry, I was desperate for a husband. Because of my desperation, I never saw the signs that the man who aggressively pursued me was not good for me as a lover, husband, or father figure and role model for my son. Despite objections from my beloved grandmother, I married him anyway. Over the years, I could hear my grandma shouting, "You are independent, so why are you going to run off and get married and become dependent on this man?" Sadly, it was years later before I finally understood her message and realized she had been correct about my situation.

Prior to becoming pregnant with my second child, because of my mother's severe and continuous drug addiction, we legally adopted my youngest brother. It was during this same timeframe that I initially discovered that my spouse was a habitual liar. Unfortunately, by the time that I realized this, I was already pregnant with my second son. Shortly thereafter, I recognized that not only was he a liar, but had the makings of a cheater too. Slowly but surely, I came to the realization that the man I married was not the man that God planned for me to marry.

As my military career continued, so did global terrorism. By the time I transitioned from being an Enlisted Soldier to a Warrant Officer, I had begun various rotations to support the Global War on Terrorism. By then, I had been married for a little over 10 years and the marriage was in serious trouble. In January 2005, my first military deployment was to Iraq. Shortly after I returned home from my deployment, his infidelity was confirmed and a child had already been conceived outside of our marriage. As far as I was concerned, mentally and emotionally, the marriage was essentially over.

Several months went by before legal separations began. Prior to my return from another temporary duty assignment, my children witnessed U-Haul trucks being parked in our driveway while our most valuable possessions were taken from our home. It wasn't until months later and during my second deployment to Iraq, that my children told me that our furniture was in an apartment occupied by my soon to be ex-husband and his girlfriend/future wife.

In December 2006, merely six days into my second military deployment to Iraq, I barely survived being killed by an Improvised Explosive Device (IED) Explosion. The IED explosion caused me to suffer from Traumatic Brain Injury (TBI), short-term memory loss, blurred vision, and hearing loss. It was during this military deployment to Iraq that my spouse filed a motion for divorce.

While home from Iraq on R&R, I finally received my copy of the final divorce decree. Upon reading the document, I noted two important things. First, the motion for divorce was sent to an unoccupied residence. Second, upon filing the motion for divorce, my spouse had completely removed my son from my custody. Much to my surprise, I discovered that I was legally no longer a custodial parent of my son. Like so many others, I was one of those Soldiers who lost custody of their children while on a military deployment. Needless to say, I immediately jumped to action and hired a lawyer who was expensive, but known to be the best. This lawyer assisted me with regaining parental custody of my son.

In January 2008, while conducting a site assessment in Iraq as we prepared for our third deployment, I scarcely survived being killed by a mortar / rocket attack. Minutes prior to the attack, I decided to delay taking my nightly shower. Within an hour or so, someone banged on my door to verify that I was alive. I learned that the rocket landed directly in front of the door of the female shower where I would have been had I taken my shower as originally planned. Had I taken that shower it would've been my last because I would have been killed instantly.

~ *Sonya LaVonka Howell Barrow* ~

In July 2009, instead of going to Iraq for my third deployment, we were rerouted to Afghanistan. By September 2009, I developed severe abdominal pain that required me to be medically evacuated from the war zone to Landstuhl Regional Medical Center (LRMC) in Germany, where I underwent exploratory abdominal surgery. Afterwards, I was redeployed to my home station. Once I recovered and healed, I was deployed back to Afghanistan.

In January 2010, I was deployed back to Afghanistan. It was during this deployment that I participated in the very first Commencement Ceremony for University of Maryland, University College (UMUC), now known as University of Maryland Global Campus (UMGC). Shortly upon my redeployment from Afghanistan, I began to suffer from unexplained swelling and unexplained weight gain.

## Surviving Medullary Thyroid Cancer

One year after returning from Afghanistan, I accepted a military assignment to Germany. Prior to this decision, my oldest son had joined the United States Army, completed Basic Training and MOS Training and had relocated to Texas. Therefore, my youngest son and I embarked on our journey to Germany alone. Years later, due to unforeseen circumstances with my mother, she became my military dependent and moved to Germany with us.

My mother became sick several months after her arrival. Because her throat was enlarged, LRMC determined that my mother required additional medical care at Walter Reed National Military Medical Center (WRNMMC) located in Bethesda, Maryland. LRMC wanted a second opinion as to whether my mother had thyroid cancer. WRNMMC determined my mother had Stage 3 Medullary and Papillary Thyroid Cancer and she underwent a total thyroidectomy.

Prior to my mother's surgery, I was advised that throat cancer was genetic, and I required medical labs and tests as well. Upon extensive lab, radiology and other tests, doctors at WRNMMC discovered that I was in the early stages of Medullary Thyroid Cancer. During December 2013, I underwent a total thyroidectomy. Upon recovery, I was advised to have both of my sons genetically tested to determine if they were also prone to develop thyroid cancer. Throughout my time being diagnosed and treated for thyroid cancer, I was still a single parent, an Active Duty United States Army Soldier and a student pursuing a Master's Degree in Cyber Security at UMUC.

Though I was always apprehensive and filled with uncertainty, I knew there was something better waiting for me. I reminded myself that *better days are coming.* So, I kept on pushing and I kept on praying. Thankfully, my mental strength is stronger than my physical strength. I know where I am going because I know my purpose in my life. I continue to move in that direction and I am highly motivated by the thoughts of endless possibilities for me and my two children.

## Finding the F.I.R.E. Within

Although I was conceived by accident, ultimately my grandmother allowed me to be born despite not being planned. Throughout my life, I was destined to be a statistic. Although the odds have always been stacked against me and never in my favor, I maintained a burning "fire" within me. My determination to defy any hindrances against me and to achieve the successes in life have always fueled this fire I so desperately want.

I overcame many obstacles in my life. Now that I am on the other side, I am able to share glimpses of my life's story with you. I hope that it will shine a beacon of hope and confidence for you and your story.

I am a survivor because I refused to give up on myself or the life I have been blessed to live. Perhaps I would not be the confident and strong-willed woman today that the little girl saw in the mirror, had I not experienced childhood traumas, teenage pregnancy, failed marriage, military deployments and other negative adversities in my life. However, by the Grace of God, I am still here. Therefore, I consistently remove negative obstructions from my path and continue to work hard to do great things and live my best life.

"*God ain't through with me yet,*" is what I tell myself daily. Reciting this quote daily prevents me from feeling hopeless, helpless or trapped in negativity. I am bursting with "***F.I.R.E.***" because I am igniting the joy and love within.

**F** = Fearless Faith

**I** = Inspiration

**R** = Resilience

**E** = Empowerment

I have the "***FIRE***" in my mind, body, and spirit. You, too, can have the "***FIRE***". All you have to do is continue to believe in yourself. I believe in you. Always remember that each day is a present, so enjoy the gift and continue to live your blessed life.

With Love,

Sonya

---

***"I can do all things through Christ who strengthens me."***

***Philippians 4:13*** *NKJV*

---

*~ Sonya LaVonka Howell Barrow ~*

# Coming Soon...

***"SHE IS ME! Defying My Life's Obstacles By Not Becoming A Statistic"*** is my memoir. My memoir will resonate with many readers who may or may not be familiar with financial hardships, drug-addicted parents, homelessness, teenage pregnancy, failed marriages, military deployments, and lots of other traumatic experiences.

My memoir will help provide clarity for the glimpse of my story that I have already shared with you.

*Sonya LaVonka Howell Barrow*

Contributing Author

# *About Sonya*

**Sonya LaVonka Howell Barrow**

Sonya LaVonka Howell Barrow is a retired U.S. Army Combat Veteran who served honorably and distinctively for over 26 years in various organizations and deployments before retiring as a *Chief Warrant Officer Five (CW5)* in November 2018.

Over the years Sonya has provided encouragement by sharing glimpses of her life's story for inspiration. She knows first-hand about childhood traumas and acknowledges that her life very well could have classified her as *just another statistic* in American society. Thankfully, Sonya did not accept this as her reality and vowed that her challenging experiences would not define her. Instead, she made the decision to overcome her circumstances and improve the trajectory of her life and her children's lives.

Following her retirement from the Army, Sonya is realizing her dream to be a published author. She is currently penning her memoir entitled,*"She Is Me! Defying My Life's Obstacles By Not Becoming A Statistic."* She hopes that her story will be a blueprint and guide that will inspire others who may find themselves faced with difficult circumstances. Sonya believes that God's grace and mercy have allowed her to overcome many obstacles and she is dedicated to inspiring and encouraging others to create the life they want rather than dwell in the one that they've already experienced.

Sonya is from Augusta, Georgia, and was raised by her beloved grandmother Mary and her mother Gail. Sonya is a graduate of the University of Maryland, University College (UMUC) with a Master's Degree in Cyber Security. Additionally, she has Information

Technology and Project Management training. Sonya is a certified **Life Coach** and has trained as a professional in the practices of *Mindfulness* and *Meditation.*

As the mother of two adult sons; Jacques and DeShon, Jr., Sonya recognizes that her purpose is to encourage others who have experienced life experiences similar to her own. She chooses to be a beacon of hope that others may need to know their past traumas do not have to define their future legacy.

When she is not writing, Sonya enjoys reading, traveling, and spending time with family and friends. Her faith, strong will, and determination helped to redefine her future.

# From Crisis to Clarity

## Bernice Johnson

*~ Bernice Johnson ~*

# From Crisis to Clarity

**By Bernice Johnson**

As a parent, you have so much unconditional love for your children, and you would do anything to ensure they are safe and out of harm's way. You want to be their protector. But what happens when that love for your child turns into unbearable pain that is completely out of your control? When your parental relationship is blown out of the water and your child becomes a person, you don't even recognize anymore. I pray my parental journey can ensure you that love conquers all. All it takes, are you getting out of the driver's seat and allowing God to take control because God can bring healing full circle when you just stay on course. Your road to recovery may not be easy but it is most definitely worth it. I want to be able to inspire you when your heart becomes so heavy, and you must dig deep inside of you to find that inner strength that allows you to fight the good fight of faith.

Imagine receiving a phone call concerning the safety of your child that literally stops your heart from beating for a split second. In November 2020, one single phone call impacted my life in a way I would have never imagined. I remember the call so clearly until it gives me chills just by going back in time to rekindle that very moment. My one and only daughter was admitted to the hospital for attempted suicide. I still can't believe it. I never would've thought something like this could happen so close to home.

Sitting at my desk, working from home during the height of the Covid-19 pandemic, my phone rang, and a woman name Brittany from a mental health facility was on the other end of the phone line. She calmly said, "We have a patient that listed you as her mom and her point of contact and I wanted you to know that she's been transported to the hospital for attempted suicide by intentional overdose, but she is alive." At that moment, my entire world froze. My heart raced and I could literally feel the rapid beats in my chest as my heart rate sped up tremendously. I felt my chest tighten as I grasped for air to breathe. My body went silently numb as my eyes filled with water and a slight tear flowed down my cheeks before the overflow of emotions consumed me. My hands began visibly shaking as the tears continued to pour down my face. There was such a huge knot in my belly that made me feel extremely nauseous. In disbelief, I felt trapped in a nightmare; my one and only daughter was admitted to the hospital for attempted suicide. Wait, what??? Attempted suicide??? How is this even possible???

Being my only daughter, I always felt she was so temperamental and spoiled. She could never accept my "No." So, I felt when I gave her what I considered "tough love" she would be in her feelings and eventually get over it. Never in a million years did I think me disagreeing and strongly voicing my opinion as well as disapproving of her life choices would cause her so much pain that she would want to take her own life. She attempted what I felt was the "unbelievable" and it shattered my heart in a million pieces. I was so heartbroken until my thoughts were too hard for me to swallow. Everything started to unravel, and I began to question myself. My mind was so cloudy, and I couldn't even think clearly. I couldn't process all these emotions at once. So, I began to ask myself, was I too hard on her? My anger creeped in and I wondered, should I even talk to her again? I even questioned if I was a bad parent? If only I had not been so judgmental and listened more and talked less that I could have probably circumvented her from trying to take her own life.

During this crisis, so many feelings bombarded me at once as I was trying to process the fact that this was real life and not just a bad dream that I would soon awaken from. So, I felt guilty, confused and so very heartbroken. A tsunami of questions continued to flood my thoughts. Was there anything I could have done differently with her as a child? What could I have changed in her childhood? The emotions of disappointment slowly started seeping in, that lead to self-blame and me asking myself a myriad of questions. I felt it must be my fault; I didn't do enough for her as a child and that I must have done something wrong, and what was happening now was all my fault. It had to be my fault, right?

~ *Bernice Johnson* ~

The generational impact from my parents filtered through me when I expressed my blunt concerns to my daughter of her life choices. I wished I had known that being so brutally honest with my daughter's life choices would have caused her so much pain, I would have taken a different approach. All I ever wanted was the best for her. I just wished I realized that her mental capacity wasn't as strong as I thought it was. Even though I consider myself to be mentally strong, and I just assumed that she also had that same mental strength. Oh, boy was I so wrong! I had no idea that she wasn't able to accept constructive criticism from anyone and, most definitely, not from me. If I could have only recognized her silent cries out for help, I may have been able to help her seek proper counseling before she took that dreadful step towards what she considered her only way out.

Over time, as I think back, I remember that there was such a roller-coaster ride of emotions leading up to the suicide attempt. There were some unspoken warning signs that I failed to recognize. Or maybe I saw them and didn't want to see them. Could this be the same child I gave birth to 27 years ago that was swaddled in a baby blanket and placed on my chest immediately after delivery? So, I feel compelled to highlight these silent cries because I now see them as signs that should have been closely observed and noted in the beginning because they could have prevented this inevitable event from taking place. Sometimes the signs for crying out for help come on gradually, and I want to highlight these signs because it could save a life if detected and addressed early, before things get too far gone. There were some days she was sad, quiet, withdrawn, isolated, easily irritated and offended, yet always tired. At times, she would have what I called a "grown person temper tantrum." She would be irate and simply mean. I honestly thought she was being dramatic and seeking attention, or simply just overreacting. As for me, there were days I found myself getting frustrated with her because I felt that she didn't have any reason to be on such an emotional rollercoaster ride because I made her life as financially comfortable as possible from childhood to adulthood. Some days, I even found myself becoming bitter, disappointed, and frustrated because I thought she was simply being selfish and acting spoiled. I mistook those telltale signs because I was blinded by my own frustration and apparently, they were red flags that I looked at as simply negative behavior. When, in actuality, she was crying out for help.

As my life during this crisis unfolded, I was nervous, and I was "walking on eggshells" as my mom would always say when things got tense. After my daughter attempted to take her own life, I simply didn't know the right way to approach her. Or did a *right way* even exist? I was terrified because that simple thought was stuck in the back of my mind; she could possibly try it again and things could turn out differently next time. Ever hit a stumbling a block? I hit an entire brick wall and didn't know what to expect from her going forward. I didn't know what to say because I didn't want to trigger her depression to cause her to down spiral again. She seemed to have many triggers when it came to me, and my "tough love." She was yet so fragile, and I was cautious to openly express myself to her. I knew as a mother, I should always be able to talk to my baby girl, but I was at a point where I didn't know how to emotionally connect with her. It was hard to accept that my bundle of joy, even though it was 27 years ago, had her innocence snatched away and her mind was so contaminated. But as her mother, I was determined to mentally and emotionally reach her because I knew my baby girl was still in there somewhere.

So, at any given time, you think that your parental relationship is in jeopardy, please take the time out to try and mend it immediately. I made a conscious decision to really change the trajectory of our relationship because I was determined to help her clear the clutter in her mind. I believed that things were going to get better, so I used the following strategies and pray they will be helpful to others who may be experiencing strain and tension in their parent-child relationships. Make sure to always use a direct approach instead of texting or having a phone conversation, take time to sit down with your child to have a face-to-face conversation with them about their emotions or concerns. Allow them to be open and honest to vent without the fear of them being judged negatively. Time is precious, so make time to take day trips just to ride and chat because it allows the both of you to have a clear mind. Create lasting memories. Try to create moments when you can sit down with them over some ice cream or their favorite dessert. Ice cream still makes my daughter one of the happiest girls in the world. Family time is important, so make dinner plans with them at their favorite restaurant or prepare their favorite meal at home so it will allow them time to openly converse with you. Most importantly, ensure them that you are there to understand what's going on with them and never there to make them feel bad about any life choices they made even if it wasn't their best choice, but it was just an opportunity for a learning experience. Make sure to explain to them that you love them so much that you simply don't want them to go through the pain that you see waiting for them on the other side of that particular choice. You must emphasize that it is not about judgement or control, but much more about the maternal protector factor that drives your response to their choices.

As my daughter and I continue to work on our relationship, I share the bad choices I made in life that helped me grow into the best version of myself because she thought I was perfect and didn't make mistakes. I ensured her I am far from perfect and will continue to make mistakes through my life journey. I now let her know that I am not disappointed in *her* even if the choice she made wasn't a choice I would I have made. I assure her that we all must live our life how we choose, and as her mother, I have set the foundation for her since childhood. I just pray that if she goes astray that she will look back on that foundation and allow it to bring her back on course.

As I continue to seek clarity in my parental relationship with my daughter, our relationship may not be where I want it to be, but it most definitely has gained great momentum from where it used to be toward where I want it to be. God ensured me that my battle was already won, but I just had to stay on course and focus on the road ahead of me because he allowed me another chance with her to get it right. God used this crisis to allow me to gain knowledge and clarity that depression is real. Your mental health is a jewel that you should always keep polished and never take it for granted. Always take time out for self-care and most importantly, take mental health breaks. It is very important to investigate and recognize warning signs of depression that loved ones may display. Constantly ask questions to see how they are feeling, pay attention to sudden or even gradually behavioral changes in your loved ones. Try your best to recognize when they are hurting or suffering in silence. Make sure to not only pray *for* your children but pray *with* your children - even when they become adults with their own children.

This crisis gave me a radical shift in faith, I decided to step out of the driver's seat and allowed God to be the driving force in my life. My daughter's crisis gave me clarity on knowing that hurt can be healed. So, when I cried out to God to take the pain away, I first thanked Him for allowing me to be my daughter's earthly mother, and I realized I had to give her back to Him because I could not carry this burden. I knew I could not fix this by myself, and I needed God to have His way and do His will. So, at that moment, I allowed God to take control and be the foundation that helped strengthen my relationship with my daughter. God reminded me of his word, ***"A time is coming and in fact has come when you will be scattered, each to your own home. You will leave me all alone. Yet I am not alone, for my Father is with me. "I have told you these things, so that in me you may have peace. In this world you will have trouble. But take heart! I have overcome the world."*** **John 16: 32-33 (NIV).**

So, I listen more and talk less. I journal my thoughts and anything negative that comes to mind while journaling; I write them down, rip them out of my journal and shred them so they are longer in my head but on paper and discarded. My journey with my daughter is far from over, but we thank God every day for giving us a second chance at love. As for her, she is actively going to therapy and has started journaling her thoughts as she works on herself. I even supply her with journals. She is learning to love herself despite what others think. As for me, I am currently seeking spiritual counseling as I continue my faith walk with God. Additionally, I am researching to find the best therapist that can help me heal from this pain. Going forward, the road to recovery may be long for me, but I made a conscious decision to find my "FOYER = Focus On Yourself Every day Regardless." I have encouraged my daughter to do the same and also recommend you FOYER as well.

*~ Bernice Johnson ~*

*Bernice Johnson*

Contributing Author

# *About Bernice*

**Bernice Johnson**

Bernice Johnson was born and raised in the country, but recently gave up *country life* to become a resident of the Capital of South Carolina in 2019. Bernice is currently a Senior Commercial Underwriter Assistant, where she supports a team of various commercial property insurance underwriters.

Bernice has devoted her life to doing her best to make her past life choices work positively for her and her three children. When depression knocked on her front door and she was afraid to answer, Bernice resolved to work on herself and now uses what she learned from the challenges she faced to help others overcome their obstacles.

She has a mindset of a perfectionist, but her life has been far from perfect. Becoming a parent at the young age of 20 years old, and now as a single mother of three, Bernice realized that she had to work on herself and build a life for her family. She developed the F.O.Y.E.R. method and has found great success in turning negative situations into positive learning opportunities for growth. F.O.Y.E.R. is an acronym for ***F****ocus* ***O****n* ***Y****ourself* ***E****very* ***day*** ***R****egardless.*

Acknowledging and recognizing that feeling of hopelessness that so often causes people to get stuck, Bernice seeks to be an inspiration to others and give them hope. She has overcome many trials and tribulations in her own life and wants to show people that they can conquer even the most difficult situations they may have encountered.

She is a *recovering workaholic* but has since slowed down to stop and smell the roses. Bernice is inspired and coached by her mentor, Fa'apepele "Pele" Hunkin, *The Vessel of Love & Positivity,* an Author, and a Global Speaker. When she is not helping others, Bernice finds great fulfillment in daily journaling.

*~ Bernice Johnson ~*

# From Depression to Determination

Mae Juarez Cervantes

# From Depression to Determination

**By Mae Juarez Cervantes**

Mmmmmm. It smells sooooo good. That delightful aroma of homemade cake will always be etched in my mind. I'll never forget the smell of my mother's homemade steamed cassava cake. It smelled so good and tasted even better. As a little girl, I wasn't the only one who loved my mother's homemade cakes. In fact, it was so wonderful that people bought it. I was her chief marketing agent! I would stroll through the town of Cateel, Davao Oriental, selling these delicious cakes. These cakes always put a big smile on people's faces.

Growing up, I had very humble beginnings. I was blessed with wonderfully supportive and devoted parents who poured their love into me. Unfortunately, they didn't have a lot of money and often struggled to make ends meet. They instilled in me that we had to work together and each do our part. In fact, I've been an entrepreneur since elementary school. I sold snacks in school so that I could make money and bring it home to my parents. One of my neighbors was selling "puto," a Filipino steamed rice cake, and I convinced her to allow me to sell it for her. She paid me a very small commission, but it was better than nothing. I wanted to make extra money so that I didn't have to trouble my parents when things came up at school that required money.

By the time I was 8 years-old I knew I was naturally an entrepreneur at heart. I remember when it all started for me. We celebrated Independence day in the Philippines and our teacher asked us to make a Philippine flag to get additional points. Many of my classmates weren't able to bring their flags, so I made many flags and sold them all. It was the first time that I earned money - and I fell in love with the idea! After I graduated from elementary school, I had a sari-sari store (a small convenience store). I got the taste of entrepreneurship on my palette and it never left me.

Of course, I knew the importance of having money. It was something my parents didn't have the luxury of being able to shield me from. My parents often had to deal with it and it was really hard for them. My mother had a business, but it went down and caused us to have extreme financial worries. We were in debt, and my parents didn't have stable jobs. They struggled for years to get back on their feet. It was definitely a tough time for us. I would silently cry when I saw my mother looking so tired. She never gave up. She washed clothes for others and cleaned their houses. It broke my heart when she wasn't treated well by a few people. She didn't deserve that, but I realized this is unfortunately what comes with poverty.

I started feeling sorry for myself and being envious of other people who seemed to be in a better position. I felt unlucky and helpless. But not my mom; she kept a friendly and hopeful spirit even though she had such a rough time. She was always reminding me to be humble, understanding, and patient. I know it hurt her that I didn't have a lot of fun times with friends. The truth of the matter is that I didn't have time for fun because, obviously, my parents needed help. I was adamant that I was going to work hard with my parents so we could have money to buy food. We were definitely in survival mode. Sadly, I started thinking that because we didn't have money; we didn't have value either. I felt like I wasn't enough.

I became somewhat of a loner and stayed to myself. I think my classmates realized this and by the time I entered high school; they started bullying me. I went to a private high school and didn't really mingle with my classmates. I preferred to stay at home, help my mom, study, and write in my diary. I didn't have many friends. In fact, my best friends were my mom and my diary. That was fine with me. I didn't feel a need to have a bunch of friends. Throughout my time in high school, I was content with just doing well in school, helping my family make ends meet, and studying. I focused on being an excellent student and it paid off for me. I received several scholarships for college.

The scholarships were very helpful. I sold snacks and other items to make extra income. Because of my work schedule and my studies, I was often tired and lonely. I became weak and vulnerable. After a while, I was introduced to some bad habits, and it became a struggle to leave them behind. I made a lot of questionable choices and decisions that weren't really in my best interest. Bad things happened to me and people seemed to take advantage of me and my desire to find a cure for my loneliness and weariness. As a result, I was angry, resentful, and bitter. I was looking for happiness in people and all the wrong things. I lost trust in humanity and felt like life was unfair. I became angry with God. With all this hatred for people in my heart, I began seeking revenge. I was definitely sad and hurting. I did not have a grateful heart. In fact, I would even say I was jealous of many of my classmates and their families. I felt like everybody was doing better than I.

Even though I had these negative feelings, I knew I had to just deal with them. I didn't really have a choice, so I pushed through my feelings and school as best that I could. I became a people pleaser and a perfectionist. As much as this caused me trouble later on, it was good for the moment because it motivated me to be an excellent student. Once I got to college, I continued to excel. I didn't consider myself to be really smart, but I was a very hard worker though. I worked so hard that I ended up making myself quite sick. The doctor told me to take a break from college and rest for at least three months because I was so sick. That devastated me! Not only was I physically sick, the thought of having to leave college made me emotionally sick. Unfortunately, I didn't have a choice. I was forced to return home to my village. I was brokenhearted and now unable to keep my scholarships; I was financially broke too!

Once I recovered and became healthy again, I decided to get a job. Having lost my scholarships, I knew I had to pay for my education. I understood it would be hard, but I was committed to change the trajectory of my life. I shared my plan with my parents and they backed my decision. I was definitely frightened, but I was also determined that I was going to do whatever it took to get my college education. I realized it was going to require a lot of hard work, but I knew I could do it. God gave me the strength I needed, and I set out to make my plan work.

Of course, I needed money to make the plan work. So, I sold a wireless internet stick to my cousin; accumulating enough money for a bus ticket and a month's allowance. My parents gave me as much pocket money as they could. I made up my mind and now I was going to do what I had to do to get back into college. I knew it would be difficult, but I also realized I had a strong support system to help me. My parents (Herculano and Annabelle), Aunt Leila, Aunt Marisa, and a few close friends helped me tremendously. I will always be grateful to them for everything they did to assist me during my time in college.

Thankfully, I was successful with my first job interview. I got the job and was able to pay for my education. I was thrilled to return to college. Fast forward to my last year. I faced many challenges and struggles. As if college wasn't hard enough on its own, something happened that really caused me significant problems. One of my professors did not put grades in for me and I could not get it resolved. Because of her negligence and the fact that I didn't notice it soon enough, forced me to retake that course, which cost me more time and money. I was about to enroll in new subjects for the next term when I realized the omission. It could have been easily resolved if I had checked it at the end of the semester. My graduation was postponed, and I was shattered. Feeling like a failure, I slipped into depression and resorted to vices such as drinking and smoking. Of course, I knew these things were not good for me, but I was trying to ease my pain. My self-esteem was badly bruised, and I was really disappointed in myself. I started to miss classes and not complete assignments. Clearly, I should be doing better and couldn't keep going down this path if I intended to graduate. I lost my focus and direction. The hatred I had buried in my heart a few years prior came to the surface again. I didn't like it and, in fact, didn't even like myself anymore.

As the bible says, this too shall pass. Thank God it did. Things finally started to get better. A classmate who was a lot older than me noticed how much I was struggling. I didn't realize it at first, but she would become my mentor. She was so concerned about me that she came to my boarding home to have a heartfelt discussion and encourage me. This was a turning point for me. She didn't give up on me and she wouldn't let me give up on myself. She took me under her wing and helped me complete my projects and get back on track. I am so grateful to her and I'm not sure where I would be if she hadn't noticed my situation and committed to help me fix it. It wasn't easy, but at least I was moving in the right direction.

One bright spot in this part of my life was that I met my partner. He reminded me of how loving and merciful God is and led me to become interested in developing a better relationship with God. As I studied the Bible and learned more about God's words, ultimately, my attention turned to *"The Old Path"* program. I watched their online videos and became captivated by their sharing of God's Words. The more I listened, the softer my heart became. I was healing and getting back to becoming the person my mother had taught me to be. My eyes were opening and so was my heart. Though my heart was opening, my mind was still very cluttered. Lost, confused, and exhausted, one night I had an emotional breakdown. It was the middle of the night. I was weeping and began to pray fervently. It was just me and God. I talked with Him and asked Him to heal me. I realized that I couldn't do it by myself, so I asked Him to give me the strength I needed to turn my life around.

I asked for God's forgiveness for all my mistakes and committed to change. I gave up all my vices and chose to forgive those who hurt me. I forgave myself and was determined to live according to God's will. Forgiveness freed me, and I am very grateful to God. It changed my life so much and allowed me to find joy.

God touched my heart and gave me a plan. I was ready to turn my life around and implement His plan, but little did I know my circumstances would change once again. This time I wasn't sick – I was a mommy! Things became tough again. By the time my son was one-year-old, I had to find a job to help my partner pay the bills and provide for our child. I couldn't be the mommy I wanted to be because I was always either on my way to work or on my way to sleep. I didn't have time to enjoy my son. He was asleep when I went to work and asleep again when I arrived home. I felt guilty that I couldn't be there for him all the time.

I would have to leave the house by 6 AM and not get back home until 7 or 8 PM. There were times when my son was awake when I went out of the house to work. He cried so hard and it broke my heart. I hated to leave him. I cried while on my commute and silently prayed to God to help me find a way to earn money and have time to take care of my son.

My mother and friends encouraged me to find an online job and start working from home. I was hesitant because I had the fear of uncertainty and failure. Then God showed me that my WHY is bigger than my fear. So, I decided to quit this challenging routine that I hated. I searched for an online job. With God's help, I was hired as a social media virtual assistant for a fitness and business coach. It was the best decision ever, and it was just in time for the pandemic!

I quickly found joy in digital marketing and invested in more training, courses, coaching, etc. to help me provide the best service. I love learning. Sharing my knowledge, skills, or being able to solve a problem is something that I am very excited about. I'm also able to spend more time with my family, and my Sonshine is seeing more of his mommy than ever before! Don't get me wrong; being a *mompreneur* definitely has its challenges.

It wasn't easy to start an online business because there are a lot of challenges and sacrifices that must be made. But it's true, that if you love what you do, you don't feel like you're working at all. I learn new things every day and it is really fulfilling when my clients are satisfied with my work, but even that comes at a price. I started noticing that a lot of fear kept rising in me. The fear of visibility, failure, rejection, and uncertainty were just a few of the things I struggled with.

I became so focused on performing well and doing everything on my own that I was almost right back in the same boat that had led me here. I got distracted by everything I felt I had to learn and lost focus on what mattered most. I worried a lot and had many sleepless nights. My limiting beliefs kept bubbling up in my mind, which caused me to suffer from imposter syndrome. It reminded me of my childhood, when I felt like I wasn't good enough. Once again, I faced that old familiar thing in my life – burnout!

Burnout is real! If you're not careful and let it linger too long, it can be a dream killer. I want to encourage you to be very intentional about fighting burnout. I have a few ideas that helped me along the way and they may help you too. It all starts with self-care. Do your best, but don't push yourself to the point of exhaustion. I cannot tell you enough how important getting your proper rest is to your overall life experience. If you're afraid, remind yourself that you are loved and you are strong. Never forget that God loves you unconditionally. Don't be afraid of taking risks. Use failures to succeed. Be willing to forgive yourself, be grateful, and always remember that you are valuable.

I've learned to set some boundaries and to protect my time and energy. Another thing that I have found to be incredibly important is to stay away from toxic people who can drain me emotionally and mentally. I guard my peace and surround myself with people who have a mindset similar to my own. Be with people who empower and encourage you. If they don't – you don't need to spend time with them. Loving someone or caring about them shouldn't be at the expense of your health and well-being. Love them from a distance. One of my favorite guiding Scriptures is, "Do everything in love." ~ 1 Corinthians 16:14.

Life is always going to have its challenges, but that's okay. Just do the best that you can do at that time. Whenever I feel stressed or worried about something, the following Scripture reminds me to be calm, let go, and let God. "And we know that in all things God works for the good of those who love him, who have been called according to his purpose." ~ Romans 8:28

I remind myself of these three important things in life; faith, hope, and love. In fact, I even incorporated them into my logo as a constant reminder in my business and my personal life. "And now these three remain: faith, hope and love. But the greatest of these is love." ~ 1 Corinthians 13:13

God gave me the ability to transform from depression to determination, making me more than a conqueror. Throughout my journey, I came to the realization that my only choice was to have the tenacity and motivation to be the best version of myself. Whatever I encountered, I had to motivate myself to think positively. Because I have been given the ability to be a blessing to others, I am now committed to making a positive difference in people's lives. I want you to have self-confidence because I have faith in you. Remember, it is not about how you started, but how you finish the race with the grace of God that truly makes you a conqueror.

~ *Mae Juarez Cervantes* ~

*Mae Juarez Cervantes*

Contributing Author

# *About Mae*

Mae Juarez Cervantes is a brand strategist, content marketing specialist, and social media mentor who helps speakers, coaches, and authors build a magnetic and profitable brand with love, confidence, and ease. She's the founder of ***Maegnetic Socials***—a social media agency that caters branding, social media marketing, and web design services.

She quit her 9-5 lifestyle because she wanted to work from home and take care of her Sonshine. It was scary for her to try something new, but she did it anyway because her dreams are bigger than her fears. She discovered digital marketing and found joy in helping others build impactful personal brands, increase brand awareness, drive traffic to their websites, generate leads, nurture existing audience, and maximize profits. She found her passion.

Mae is from Cateel, Davao Oriental Philippines. She's a graduate of the Bachelor of Secondary Education Major in English and Multimedia Arts Major in Graphic Design. She studied digital marketing at Digital Marketer and focused on branding and social media marketing.

She enjoys reading, engaging online, and most of all, Karaoke singing with family and friends.

She experienced many challenges in life since she was a child that, along the way, helped her learn more and grow. She has struggled with perfectionism, procrastination, and people pleasing.

She experienced many challenges in life since she was a child that helped her learn more and grow. She has struggled with perfectionism, procrastination, and people pleasing.

*~ Mae Juarez Cervantes ~*

However, she managed to overcome those challenges by learning to accept herself for who she is and learning to love herself for who she is.

As a mom, she feels like she has a lot of responsibilities and cares so much on others that she forgets about herself. She became too hard on herself that led her to burn out. Limiting beliefs and fears crept in but she never gave up on trying.

It wasn't easy for her to show up online. She's an introvert and tends to worry a lot and overthink situations. She prefers to be working behind the scenes, but she was willing to try something unfamiliar.

She decided to become a better version of herself by exposing herself to the world and using her gifts or skills to help others. She became intentional about her own purpose. She became kinder to herself and embrace imperfections.

She's a believer in the power of change. She believes that we all have the ability to make a difference in this world, and that if we want to see the world change for the better, we need to start by changing ourselves. She chose to show up for herself unapologetically. She was recognized as one of the TOP 50 Pioneers of Change by Women of Dignity Magazine. She continues to inspire and encourage others, especially moms like her, to do what they love, serve with love for others, love themselves, and above all, love the Almighty God.

# Conquer Your Fears: Five Steps to Success

Coach Teon Singletary

# Conquer Your Fears: Five Steps to Success

**By Coach Teon Singletary**

Every morning, I wake up and say, "I am greatness made from Greatness." Why? Because today is a great day to be alive. Now, not every day is great. We all travel on this life journey. And on this journey called life, we will have some troubles and issues that will come our way. Some fear will enter into our lives. How many of us can say that we have some fears that are holding us back from reaching our greatness? Perhaps that's you. However, I believe you have the potential inside of you to conquer your fears. In this chapter, I am going to provide you with the five steps you can use to conquer your fears. Make sure you have a pen and paper to take notes. I'm about to share some things with you that will change your life for the better. Say out loud to yourself, "I am greatness made from Greatness. And today is a great day to be alive." Before we go into the first step to conquer your fears and achieve success, I want to share with you a story.

## Facing Fears

There I was, just arriving at a new high school in 9th grade. I was on lunch break from class. In the JROTC Parade field were some cadets with a rifle in their hands, spinning and throwing it up in the air, catching it and spinning it behind their backs.

I remember this moment vividly, and I made this statement, "I want to be part of that team." What they were doing was beautiful to me. They called themselves Drill Masters. And in order to join that drill team, you had to first join the JROTC Program. Now, you had a choice to do PE or join JROTC. Yeah, that was an easy answer for me at the time. I went to JROTC.

On the first day of the program, we were in formation outside. It was a little chilly that particular morning. A man was at the doorway, and it felt like he was only *mean mugging* me. The cadet in charge of the formation guided us newbies into the building to our prospective classrooms. We recited a cadet creed and then we sat down. Then, that same man with the *mean mug* came charging in the room and started talking to us and that turned really quickly to yelling. I said to myself, "Ok, maybe I'm in the wrong place. I don't remember signing up for the military." Fear immediately entered into my heart. I was ready to get out of there.

The class session went on and before the bell rung, he asked the question I was waiting for: "Who wants to join the Drill Team?" I immediately raised my hand and asked with a big smile, "Is that the guys with the rifles?" He looked back at me with an evil smile and said, "You are correct; you want to join?" I nodded my head yes, not knowing what I was getting myself into, because the first practice was right after school that same day.

So, there I was at practice and they gave me this rifle and I almost dropped it because it was so heavy. I looked at them, then at the rifle, back at them, back at the rifle, back at them again, and said, "You want me to spin this? Are you crazy?" They said with a grin on their faces, "Yes and yes."

**Ok, ok, ok, I really did not sign up for this.**

For the next couple of weeks, they only taught us basic movements and exercises with the rifle. No spinning or throwing in the air at all. I was starting to get frustrated. I joined to spin the rifle; not to march around with my arm and shoulder muscles hurting. I did not sign up for this. As soon as I started thinking this way, the very next week, they began to teach us basic rifle spinning and throwing movements. See, they were conditioning our bodies to be able to perform these difficult movements. That's preparation.

Soon, I found myself practicing my craft during my lunch breaks on the JROTC parade field. I was trying to become the best Drill Master. Guess what, I did and I still am. That focus and determination provided me the courage to join the military when I was a *junior* in high school in 2004. Now, I am an Officer in the Army National Guard as we speak and time-to-time I still perform rifle drill shows at different events.

The moral of the story is this: sometimes we are not going to completely understand what we sign up for. However, if we stick with our decisions, greatness is waiting for us on the other side. The goal is to not give up on what you want to achieve. You must persevere to the end. Persistence produces results.

## Awareness

The first step to success is you have to be aware of your fears. Why? Because awareness is key. You cannot conquer your fear if you are not first aware of your fear. When I first joined the military, my fear was the Drill Sergeants. They immediately placed fear in my heart, just like the instructor in JROTC.

**" Fear is just false evidence appearing real."**

I thought those sergeants were my fear; however, it was false evidence. The Drill Sergeant's goal is to make you fear them. With that fear, they use it to break you down. Once they do that, their mission changes to building you up to become the best soldier you can possibly be.

There were plenty of times I wanted to give up and quit. Getting four to six hours of sleep every night, waking up 5 o'clock in the morning, and running everywhere we went was starting to wear me out. Sometimes I would wake up *toeing the line,* wondering when I got up and how I got there. Now, I can admit those were some funny times. I must say, they definitively were not funny at the time.

There was a turning point for me, and I can remember this like it was yesterday. I found myself lying in my bed thinking, "Why am I here and why do I fear the Drill Sergeants so much?" I began to analyze the situation. To my finding, I realized that I was there because I wanted to better myself and get away from the poverty mindset. I was raised in poverty and had a lot of limiting beliefs. My goal was to change that. I also realized that I should not fear the Drill Sergeants because they are human just like me.

## Preparation

Once you realize what your fear is, then and only then, you are able to complete step two. Which is to prepare yourself. See, preparation is also key. And preparation starts with your mind. You have to create the mindset to win. There is a lion or lioness, lying dormant, waiting for you to let it roar. My preparation was to work on my mind; mentally, spiritually, and physically. When I came to this realization, everything changed. I begin to enjoy my time in *basic training* and learn everything I could from the Drill Sergeants. I also began to reach back and use the tools I was given when I was in JROTC. See, I was made and prepared for this moment. I just had to realize it.

The more I submitted myself to the training, the more I grew. When I failed and fell face first to the ground, I got back up and did it again. With every blood, sweat and tear moment, I got stronger and stronger. Every obstacle and training event were preparing me for life in the military. What's your *Drill Sergeant* within your life?

## Believe

Step three is to believe in yourself. The Drill Sergeants were my fear, and I knew that. But I also knew that I had superpowers. I had to believe in myself and my capabilities. As a child, I was taught that I was built to never give up, never give in, and always persevere to the end. Believing in myself and my capabilities continue to be my superpowers.

What superpowers do you have that you can use to conquer your fears?

Believing in myself and my capabilities provided me with the confidence to endure. When I was the Platoon Guard for my group of 30+ recruits like me, I had to believe that I had the leadership skills to lead them each and every day. Which, of course, I did. I was the Battalion Commander for the JROTC program my *senior* year and I had the capabilities to lead. I just had to remind myself of this fact.

Les Brown says that, "Too many of us are not living our dreams because we are living our fears." Sometimes you will question yourself. Sometimes you will ask the question, "Why?" I want you to know that when your *why* is strong enough, you will fight through your fears. Eric Thomas says that "You've got to want it as bad as you want air to breathe." Fear makes us second guess ourselves. What I want you to do is this: "**F**ace **e**verything **a**nd **r**ise." John Maxwell says this, "Effective leadership requires the ability to stand up, stand out, and the conviction to do it." Again, I ask you, why are you afraid?

You've got to have this thing call *grit.* Day in and day out, dig deep for that grit, for that lion inside of you, to get up every day and do it over and over again each day for the rest of your life.

Say this to yourself, "I believe in me." This thing is a process. And it is a scary process. However, you can do it. Believe in yourself and believe that you have the ability to reach the finish line.

*~ Coach Teon Singletary ~*

## The Process

When you are able to believe in yourself, you are able to move to step four. Which is trust the process. See, the process is what's going to stretch you to the next level, to become bigger and better. It's the process that will help you to become the person you need to be in order to master your fears.

No one is stopping you. The only person that is stopping you is *you.* Why are you stopping yourself? Let me tell you something, "Success is not when you achieve it, success happens when you take the first step towards that achievement." My first step was when I decided to join the JROTC Program. When I did, I was fearful; however, I faced it head on. This first step gave me the chance to do something different. Joining the Drill Team gave me the opportunity to learn and grow. Joining the military gave me the opportunity to create a better life for myself and future family.

There is one common denominator is this. That brings us to the final step. Are you ready for step five?

## TAKE ACTION NOW!

One of the things that we learn within the Maxwell Leadership Team is this: Do it afraid. Jump and grow your wings as you fall. You have to have faith that everything is going to be ok. All odds may be against you. It's even possible that Murphy's law may kick in and everything that can go wrong will go wrong. Whatever the case may be, you must face your fears and take action now. When you take action on something you are supposed to, the way forward will become clear to you. This is something I had to learn personally.

As my military career began to build momentum with every small win, I found myself thinking about how can I better myself and others more. That's when I decided to embark on a self-development journey. I knew reading was an issue for me. This was an area I needed tremendous help in. To be honest, I never read a book from cover to cover until I was overseas in 2012. I regret the lost opportunities I had to when I was younger. I wish I had done a lot more reading and developed stronger reading skills. I try to laugh at my stupidity for not taking action on reading, but know it's not funny. I really do wish I had read more. However, that is history. Now, I have read close to one hundred books. How? Because I took action on my shortfall. Now, I even write my own books!

## My Growth Period

When I was younger, reading was not a strong point for me. I feared reading in front of people because I was not good at it, and I stuttered. Being picked on by students and teachers didn't help me to face that fear. It wasn't until I was introduced to a marketing business in college that encouraged and empowered me to read. It also taught me that coaching is important as well. This marketing business was Amway. The learning system they encouraged us to tap into was the Leadership Team Development. It increased my awareness of why I was where I was, and the way in which to get to where I wanted to be in life.

I followed the five steps above without even realizing it at that time, but they got me to the point I am at now. Once I was aware of why I was where I was, I began to prepare myself every day to face my fear of reading. I started small by reading a few pages at a time with the belief that I could do it. Trusting the process was fundamental during these early stages. And by taking this small action every single day, I grew a love for reading. At the end, I faced my fear of reading and I'm thankful that I did. It allowed me to become the man that I am today.

If you are aware of your fear, you can prepare yourself. Part of preparing yourself is believing in yourself. When you believe in yourself, you have the ability to trust the process. When you have this embedded in your DNA, you will have the courage to take action now and your results will be conquering your fears.

When you don't conquer your fears, you are causing someone else not to conquer theirs. Your bravery can help someone reach their greatness. It is time for you to remove that fear, allow your greatness to shine, and show the world you can't be stopped. This takes strong faith and hard work.

## The Next Step

In the Bible, ***James 2*** tells us that *faith without works is dead.* With this statement, I have three things I would like to share with you. How you apply these concepts in your life will determine your movement toward conquering your fears.

## Step Out in Faith

The first step is everything - perhaps the most important step of all. Just like a baby, once you take that first step, the rest is history. If you want to change your life for the best, take the first step in faith. Whatever your first step may be, just take it. It could be writing gratitude statements every morning and night. It could be defining or redefining your purpose and core values. It could even be seeking out a mentor or coach to assist you within your growth walk. I had to do all of the above. You need to just take action and step out in faith.

## Follow the Process

Above, I told you to trust the process. After you trust the process, you now have to follow it through and through. Everything in life has a process that you must follow. How well you follow that process will determine the outcome of your future. Just like a caterpillar, you have to follow the process to become that beautiful butterfly. Once you face your fears and learn all you can within the season that you are in, it is time for you to level up to a greater and better you. However, you have to follow the process. Within every process, there are lessons that we must learn to grow ourselves. When we decide to skip steps, we miss out on learning something we need to know for the next step. Trust and follow the process. It will do more good than harm.

## Be Willing to Learn & Grow

When you have the spirit of always learning, your perspective on life changes. Willingness to learn helps you to move from a fearful mindset to a growth mindset. Brian Herbert made this statement, "The capacity to learn is a gift. The ability to learn is a skill. The willingness to learn is a choice." Will you choose to be persistent in your willingness to learn and grow? If you do this, I guarantee you will learn how to conquer your fears and grow even more.

Again, say to yourself, "I am greatness made from Greatness. And today is a great day to be alive."

~ *Coach Teon Singletary* ~

Yes, you will have people that will not support you in conquering your fears or they may even try to stop you. I like to call those folks the naysayers and dream crushers.

**"Let your naysayers become your motivators."**

Some of those people will be your family and friends. They may have genuine concern for you, however, do not allow those concerns to steal and push you away from your dreams. Some may try to hinder you from your growth. What you have to do is push through and persevere with concrete action. When you decide to walk this walk, I will see you at your peak on the mountain top.

Before you leave, I want to share with you some tools that will change your life for the best.

- 12 Month Leadership Newsletter - **https://bit.ly/TSLeadershipNewsletter**.
- 12 Month Building Stick-to-itiveness - **https://tsle.leadingthebest.com/BSTE0001.**
- Online training - *"Five Steps To Success"* - Email a photo of this book to bless@teonsingletary.com, and I will grant you free lifetime access. Guess what, the five steps are above, however, more content is available.
- Follow me on Facebook, Instagram, and Twitter **@teonsingletary.**
- Visit the site, **www.teonsingletary.com**, for another free gift on the *15 Laws of Growth* taught by my mentor and coach, John C. Maxwell, himself.

I genuinely want to see you succeed. The question is, will you seize this opportunity and conquer your fears? The greater you is waiting for you to move. Be great in you and the things that God has empowered you to be, do, and have in life.

*-Written and copyrighted by Coach Teon Singletary, April 29, 2022*

*Coach Teon Singletary*

Contributing Author

# About Coach Teon

A South Carolina Army National Guard Soldier and Executive Director with the John Maxwell Team, Teon Singletary brings magnetic energy while inspiring you to live the best life you can.

Teon believes that you have the potential to be great. Using practical systems and strategies, his passion is supporting driven leaders and speakers who desire personal, empowering coaching to gain clarity so they can lead. Having served in the military 17+ years and having led thousands of people to excellence with precision, Teon's coaching ability has developed into a useful, compassionate and *no bs* way of helping people get what they want.

He's known as ***"The Coach":***

- Coaching leaders to level up

- Coaching individuals to inspire their lives

- Coaching speakers to spark audiences

- Coaching entrepreneurs for excellence

Teon's favorite saying is: *"You don't know what you don't know and in order to go up, you must grow up."* The power of choice is yours.

*~ Vanessa A. Simmons ~*

# Be Filled With Faith Again

**By Vanessa A. Simmons**

It's easy to look at your situation right now; your hurt, pain, and grief. It's easy to identify the things that are going wrong in your life and wonder, "Why is this happening right now?" It's easy to feel like there are things manifesting in front of your face that you don't understand and don't desire. It's easy to look at your current situation and say that everything is going wrong and nothing is going right. It's easy to find yourself falling into the *"woe is me"* trap. But it takes strength, courage, and wisdom to look at your circumstances and find the good, the purpose, and the lesson in them. On these things are we commanded to keep the focus of our thoughts, lest we drown in the stormy seas of life and be overtaken!

It was late June of 2021. I was still riding high on the wave of achievement after being selected to *speak and close* the last Les Brown Power Voice Summit. I finally opened up and shared with the world how my bout with postpartum depression and psychosis left me hospitalized and over medicated to the point that I almost lost my life. It was a really scary time. Recalling these memories brought up a lot of unresolved trauma that I was carrying about going to the Emergency Room. I found it troubling to rely on chemicals that had not been thoroughly tested for a significant period of time, rather than relying on trusted natural remedies and herbs to boost our immune system. San Diego was going through another shut down. I was homeschooling our children and managing my business from home while my husband's job was considered essential. We made the conscious decision not to vaccinate because we didn't trust the process or the safety measures used to test the vaccine's ability to fight and prevent the spread of the virus. We were also highly skeptical of the ways it was being covered in the mainstream media. When we turned to social media to gain perspective from real life experiences, in real time, from real people. There were so many people experiencing extreme side effects. We decided to trust the ability of our own bodies to build a strong immune system with vitamins, minerals, exercise, and getting outside in the sun. This was our source of good health during these uncertain times.

We trained Jiujitsu multiple times a week to sweat out the toxins created by day to day stress. Some of the ways we promoted health internally was focusing on the core vitamins that were used to prevent the virus from spreading. Vitamin D was crucial and recommended, especially for people of color. We started implementing Sea Moss, a plant that contains high amounts of vitamin D and minerals, into our diet by putting it in our daily smoothies and even taking spoonfuls of it alone when we had a runny or stuffy nose. It helps to fight mucus buildup and helps to remove mucus from the body. In our research, we learned about the body's alkaline levels and the foods that can negatively or positively affect them. It was a simple concept to understand: acidic food and drinks lead to mucus buildup, the mucus buildup leads to all kinds of different infections, and the prolonged infections can lead to disease over time. This knowledge and understanding really changed our mindset around healthy food. So naturally, we took action and applied this knowledge to our diet. Changing our diet from regular dairy, meat, and eggs (which are very acidic foods) to a plant-based diet of smoothies, plant-based milk and cheese, sprouted bread, and more fruits and vegetables like watermelon, avocados and mushrooms enabled us to pursue a more alkaline efficient diet. We also removed all refined flour and sugars from our diet because we learned that these processed foods had the ability to rapidly lower our immune system while simultaneously increasing mucus buildup.

Every morning I prepared smoothies with almond milk, sea moss, peanut butter, plant protein, ginger root, turmeric root, and a large portion of frozen fruit. I served the smoothie with one piece of sprouted bread with peanut butter. That was our breakfast routine. Although the smoothies were delicious, It was difficult with three children to remove sweets and bread from our diet. However, we made it a point to have conversations with them about our food choices and what it means in the midst of a global pandemic. We really had our bases covered. Something that I kept seeing online was that stress, fear, and anxiety could also lower your immune system. However, admittedly, I had not yet fully processed this information and applied it in wisdom to my day-to-day routines. As we began to move into mid-June, things felt like they were really beginning to flow. Every morning I started my day at 5 a.m., being filled with faith in the presence of my Creator through scripture reading and meditation. I started working on developing an app for my online community, but I was torn because I really wanted to focus on writing my first book. After a couple of weeks, I was feeling like the app was a great new way to stay connected to my community, but I kept getting stuck on the *how*. I realized I was overthinking it. I wanted it to be perfect, and I wanted everyone to be impressed with the content, but I was dealing with all of the details in my head. I was trying to figure out the best day to launch, the best price to launch, and all the specifics that were needed. All the overthinking did was lead me into overwhelm about the particulars. My deepest desire was to serve my community, but my biggest problem was working through the details without the necessary faith to keep me moving forward! Deep, unresolved fear set in as my business went into a period of bringing in no monthly income in July. I was out of ideas because I had spent my emotional reserves on managing this fear of the unknown. I started to feel so empty inside. I started to believe that it was an impossible endeavor. What I needed was to be filled with faith once again, but instead, I chose to stay stuck in a mindset of worry. I didn't really believe that I could complete my goal of writing my first book. So building the app became a huge distraction from my deepest desire and my health recognized that!

On the 4th of July, my husband and I planned a nice, quiet stay-at-home barbeque with our children. We didn't go out; we ordered in. We enjoyed the day and watched a movie together as a family, but by the end of the night a headache started to come on really strong. I figured I was tired from all of the organizing and cooking, so I decided to stay home from Jiujitsu the next morning. My husband went alone and by the time he came back, I wasn't feeling well. The children were on summer vacation at this point, so my husband suggested that I take the day off. Unfortunately, by the time he came to bed that evening, I had started to feel worse. At that time, I had no real symptoms specific to coronavirus other than the lingering headache from the previous day. The next day I was completely unable to get out of bed! My husband went to work and asked the children to look out for me. He kept in contact with them by phone throughout the day to check in and see how I was doing. However, by the middle of the day, my temperature started rising. By the time he had gotten home from work, he found me with a fever of 101° so he ran to the store to get some medicine for the fever. We all started to wonder what was going on and what I should do. However, the one thing I did not want to do was go back to the hospital. I feared I would be treated like another number or body in need of their beds. I definitely didn't want that. The Covid situation had the hospital Emergency Rooms all over the nation stretched so thinly that I knew it would be impossible for me to receive quality care. I told my husband that no matter what happened; I was not going to the hospital. I was not taking any chances with a worldwide pandemic.

It was 13 years prior when I had found myself fighting for my life from inside of a body bag. Yes, you read that right. I was put in a body bag while I was still alive! But, that is another chapter of my life. With the memory of that traumatic experience still fresh in my mind, I avoided going to the hospital. We did our research, armed ourselves with the knowledge to fight for the outcome we wanted, changed our diet, and decided to get through this without hospital intervention. Now it was time to put it all into practice and *prove that we believed* in what we prepared for. It didn't matter to me how much it would cost us to get natural remedies and the herbs that were being recommended. We started taking a high dose of vitamin C and zinc a few times a day. We stayed vigilant and consistent. My husband had to think quickly and make some hard choices when my fever became stubborn and didn't want to break. I realized that I was dehydrated and had been constipated for several days. I believed that if I could just move my bowels, the fever would break. My husband was desperate to bring my temperature down. He bought me some stool softener and electrolytes. He started taking off all of my clothes and stripped me down to my bra and underwear. He packed my body in ice and turned on the fan to cool me down as fast as possible. The dehydration led to the constipation; the constipation led to the fever, and the fever left me helpless. I even developed vertigo and was unable to walk or stand without help! Days after the fever finally broke, we went to get tested for Covid. Both of us tested positive, but my husband was asymptomatic. I was so weak that I stayed in bed for another seven days.

One morning as I was sleeping, something in my Spirit spoke and said, "Get up!" It was around 5 a.m. which was my usual time of rising. The command was so strong and bold that I responded immediately. I was determined to get back to my morning meditations in the presence of my Creator. I needed to be filled again with the faith that kept me going strong. Sometimes life comes at you fast!!! You might not feel ready to respond, but if you don't it can mean life or death. Making decisions during difficult times can feel impossible, but they are necessary. It's in these situations that your inner strength shows up. You have within you everything that is required to move strategically through the storms of life. There's power in the belief that you will never be given more than you can bear. You have to dig down deep within and realize that you can never fold to fear. These challenges will help you to identify that there is a purpose for your life here on earth. Without faith, it doesn't matter what you do - you must take action to prove that your faith is real! Planning to launch an app, even though my true desire was to write my first book, was a huge distraction. It left me feeling stuck and unavailable emotionally to my husband and children. I fell into a low frequency of fear and anxiety. Remember, stress, fear, and anxiety can suppress immunity. Needless to say, the immunity protection I needed to fight off COVID was compromised by my fear. It was not only the food I filled my body with that protected me, it was also the food I used to fill my soul. I allowed myself to get out of alignment. I filled myself with negative emotions like doubt, worry, and fear instead of filling myself with the one thing that had been protecting me all along - faith! Sometimes, you have to make a decision to let go of your fears and concerns to let in faith and courage.

Hold up your shield of faith, take a firm stand against your inner critic and self-doubt. Mentally push yourself away from that dangerous door of fear. If you aren't careful, the door of fear can lead you to a point of no return. Get up out of fear and move forward. This is what I encourage you to do when you encounter these life-or-death situations. Visualize yourself returning to a place of alignment with your Creator. Your strength will be restored as you tap into the faith that is hidden within you. Faith is an internal strength, it is your superpower, and your birthright. It will allow you to overcome every single battle that you face to win the war of life! You can, you will, and you must overcome fear and anxiety with faith, hope, and love. So, I say to you now, "Be filled with faith, once again!" to pursue your deepest desires and achieve every goal in your future.

*Vanessa A. Simmons*

**Contributing Author**

# About Vanessa

In 2014, Ghanaian-American mother and photographer, Vanessa Simmons authored the Normalize Breastfeeding® movement to address the taboo of public breastfeeding in modern society. Her mission was to document diverse variations of normal infant feeding, across cultures and delivery methods of human milk.

Through Simmons' viral blog, her photographic speaking tour, philanthropy, and artistic inspiration; she mobilized and motivated thousands of women to share their breastfeeding photos on social media. After a very successful first year, she reached out to the Mayor of San Diego to proclaim June 27th the International Day to Normalize Breastfeeding, in support of the worldwide anniversary event!

As a Certified Lactation Educator Counselor and Certified Blactivist, Vanessa Simmons, is now speaking out at conferences and events across the country to eliminate general miseducation around the topic. On the Normalize Breastfeeding podcast, she interviews guests about experiences, advocacy, and activism within the infant feeding community worldwide.

As a public speaker, Simmons is focused on transforming the modern mindset around the natural, yet difficult task of breastfeeding. Vanessa trains lactation professionals to better understand and connect with millennial families online. She creatively motivates and inspires families to be mindful that this is a time to be cherished, and although fleeting, it is also a time to reinvent what will be acceptable for feeding generations of the future.

Simmons resides with her supportive husband and three children in San Diego, CA.

# F.L.Y.

# First Love Yourself

## Fa'apepele "Pele" Hunkin

## Featured Author

# F.L.Y. ~ First Love Yourself

**By Fa'apepele "Pele" Hunkin**

Christmas is always a very exciting time for my family. It's usually a very active day. I absolutely love Christmas Day. We have so much fun and really take time to enjoy every moment of the day. Our Christmas tradition is to bring it in with the story about Jesus. We generally gather around the coffee table filled with snacks and drinks to celebrate and share why we are grateful. It's one of my favorite holidays because I take time out to tell my children how grateful I am to have them. My children are more significant to me than what life gives me. They are truly my *WHY*!!! After we lost their father 16 years ago to a tragic accident, we have become closer than ever. We celebrate everything!!

We had been looking forward to celebrating because this year; we had a special bonus; Christmas was on a Saturday so we were planning to celebrate the entire weekend. Unfortunately, this Christmas was different from any other one I ever had. It was Christmas Day, but I wasn't excited at all. My head hurt so badly that I couldn't think. It was the worst headache I had ever experienced. I was in so much pain that I was actually scared. My chest clenched, my heart was racing quickly, and I was in excruciating pain. I honestly thought my life was about to end. There was no question, I was in a medical crisis, a life-or-death situation. I couldn't even get out of the bed. I started to realize that I was fighting for my life and I was losing. Even though I didn't want them to worry, I knew I had to get my kids to help me.

I didn't have enough strength to yell loud enough for my kids to hear me. Instead, I sent a text message in our family chat group, asking them to grab the blood pressure cuff so I could find out what my blood pressure reading was. My two youngest daughters, Bella and Torie, hurried up the stairs in response to my text. As Torie was putting the cuff on my arm, she remarked, "We need to take you to the hospital, Mom. You don't look good." I put on my brave, *I'm okay face* and told them not to worry. Even though I was feeling terrible and I knew I was in trouble, I just grinned and instructed her to put the cuff on my left arm. I realized that I had to assure them that I was okay or they would panic. I didn't want them to worry. As we waited for the reading, I just smiled and told them I was okay. She pushed the start button on the cuff. The cuff tightened around my arm. It seemed like it was taking forever. Then it released, showing I had a blood pressure reading of 183/120!!! "What? Did you say *183/120*?" I thought to myself, this cuff must be broken; there's no way it's that high. Well, the cuff was fine, but *I* was not!

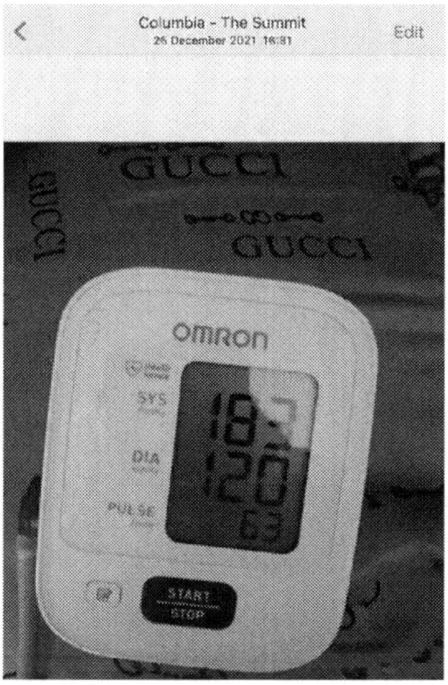


Bella and Torie had troubled expressions as they remarked, "Mommy, you need to be taken to the hospital since that level is extremely high!" I didn't respond. Instead, I requested that they give me my blood pressure medication. As I waited for the medicine to start working, I was too weak to get up. The thought of going to the hospital was making me feel even worse. I knew I didn't have the strength to get out of the bed. I laid there, feeling helpless, and began to pray. "Father God, I know you're not done with me because I have work to do, so if You could kindly give me one more chance to get my life straight, I promise I will be Your servant for life." I then glanced up at the ceiling and lifted my hands. The girls were expecting me to get ready to go to the hospital, but all I could do was outstretch my hands to the Lord. The girls looked at me, saying, "Really; you're not going to the hospital, Mommy?" Once again, I didn't reply as I just lay in bed. I could feel the warmth of God's love in my heart while I waited for the medicine to take effect. It was such a calming feeling - like the one I have read about and heard about so many times before; that *peace beyond understanding.* I just continued to lie there. I felt, deep in my heart, that I was going to be okay. I fell asleep waiting for the medicine to bring my pressure down.

When I finally awoke from my sleep, the girls told me they kept checking on me and that I had slept for several hours. I felt better when I woke up, but I still wasn't feeling like myself. I hated to admit it, but I knew I needed medical attention. The truth is that I knew the Emergency Room was going to be exceptionally busy because it was a Saturday and it's always busy on the weekends. But, this wasn't just another Saturday, it was Christmas Day! Of course, my thought was for my lovely children, who are my absolute "WHY" in life, but I just couldn't bring myself to go to the ER. A new wave of Covid was raging, and the hospitals were overflowing. I was afraid that going to the ER would be a mistake. I looked to the Lord, and I asked Him to bless me, keep me, and help me. I had faith that I would be fine if I decided to just stay in bed and rest. I promised to make an appointment on Monday with my doctor.

When I arrived at the doctor's office first thing Monday morning, I was still not feeling well, so I asked the doctor for a complete physical, which included bloodwork. What I found out would change the rest of my life. The doctor told me I was in "bad shape." It was no surprise to me that I was out of shape, but it was quite alarming to find out that it was my heart that was really the problem. So, I said to myself, "So, wait, I'm *out of shape* and *in bad shape* at the same time?" I'm trying to make light of it a little bit right now, but it really isn't a laughing matter at all. I was diagnosed with an incurable disease! I asked myself, how does this happen? The doctor informed me that I had mild atherosclerosis and that my cholesterol level was ridiculously high as well. It was 445, more than twice what it should be.

According to the Mayo clinic, atherosclerosis is the buildup of fats, cholesterol, and other substances in and on the artery walls. This buildup is called plaque. The plaque can cause arteries to narrow, blocking blood flow. The plaque can also burst, leading to a blood clot. Although atherosclerosis is often considered a heart problem, it can affect arteries anywhere in the body. Atherosclerosis puts one at risk for a heart attack or stroke. It cannot be cured, but it can be treated. The doctor explained that healthy lifestyle habits can help go a long way to minimize the harmful and potentially deadly effects.

Given the fact that my children have already experienced the loss of their father, it didn't take me long to make the choice to give it everything I have to fight this destructive disease. As I previously mentioned, my children have always been my *WHY* for everything I strive to do and this was no different. I have been through many challenging things in my lifetime and I am no stranger to obstacles and loss. I often say that my journey is one of grief and losses. The good thing is that I have a heart for it. The Lord has built me for the journey.

A few years ago, I was facing another trial in my life and doing my best to conquer a very difficult situation. I did some soul searching and figured out that at the root of many of my problems was that I loved others more than I loved myself. I began to do the hard work of reflection and self-assessment. I vowed to work on myself and was very intentional about it. I realized that I loved others and loved them so hard that I didn't leave enough love for myself. I acknowledged that this had been the toxic theme of my life and that I had to make do the necessary inner work to learn to love myself more. I created an acronym to help me remember this. I called it *F.L.Y.* which stood for *First Love Yourself.* I'm still a work in progress. Every now and then, I forget how important it is to F.L.Y. But when I was thinking about my current situation, I realized I had to once again get serious about my desire to F.L.Y.

When I first implemented F.L.Y. it was about the relationships in my life. Now, I recognized that I had to carry it over to every aspect of my life. I had to love myself enough to do what was best for me as far as my health goes. After talking with the doctor and seeing the pictures of my heart, I knew I had to choose to be healthy first, before I could do anything for my children or for myself. I love myself enough to commit to my health and my children. I'm not going to lie, I used to eat rice and bread every day and several times a day at that. I was drinking a lot of wine and even more soda, which was obviously not good for my health. I had created some awful habits which included eating a full meal sometimes as late as 1 or 2 in the morning and then going right to sleep.

I knew I had to make some major changes in my lifestyle. I decided to stop drinking alcohol and soda altogether, eat fewer fats and to reduce the amount of rice and bread in my daily diet. Another decision I made was to stop eating a full meal late at night, so I gave myself an 8 pm curfew for eating. This is my lifetime commitment to myself as I continue to F.L.Y. Thankfully, through the grace of God, I now love Pele more than ever!

I must admit that despite life's adversity, I have always learned to be grateful in all circumstances. Being diagnosed with mild atherosclerosis made me more thankful for life because it warned me about how fragile life can be and taught me how I need to I live my life. I often say that some of the most challenging situations we deal with are the very things that make us stronger. This diagnosis has once again proven that to me.

January 1st, 2022, New Year's Day, marked the beginning of my new healthy lifestyle. It was the day I implemented this lifetime commitment I call F.L.Y. This was not a resolution to me, it was a promise I made to God, my children, and myself. Understanding that how I live my life is about the choices I make, I will do everything in my power to make better choices and to be faithful to God and the life He has given to me. This is not optional for me. I have to love myself enough to make the hard choices, even when I'd rather do something else.

It's been eight months since I began this rebirthing process and I can honestly say it's been the best thing I ever did for myself. If I had to summarize it in one word, I would say this journey has been simply *breathtaking*. True to who God is, He changed the lifestyle that was *taking my breath away* from me and stealing my health to one that is *breathtaking* and building a lifestyle where I can live life to the full and live it more abundantly. I've realized my value and how much I'm worth, along with embracing all the imperfections that molded me into the beautiful authentic person I am today.

In life, we are so quick to blame our circumstances and others for what we think is going wrong, but we fail to evaluate the inner person. I want you to understand, this journey called life is an inside job; we can all examine ourselves and become the best versions of ourselves. I encourage you to look closely at yourself and not be afraid to keep evaluating until you find the beautiful you - the you that you can live with and be happy with. Ask yourself questions that will challenge you to be the better you. You have the courage and the power to overcome anything because God blessed you with the strength to make it through in life.

**Strategies That Helped Me Become a Conqueror**

I want to share with you some of the strategies that worked for me to help me as I embarked on this journey to F.L.Y.

*Allowing God to be the foundation of my life:* I believe a crucial stage in our path is accepting God as the sole source of our existence. Although I've had plenty of instances where I've wanted to quit, I want to reassure you that these difficult days are only temporary because our God is all powerful. With that being said, ask yourself the following question. Who is the cornerstone of your life? In my estimation, God is our best plan's guide and will give us hope for surviving and thriving in life. With all that I was going through, the love, mercy, and the grace of God carried me through.

The effectiveness of prayer and God's consistency with His Word inspire me. When our heart's desires align with His will, He continues to bless us. Recognize that opportunities may arise and that you must show faith and trust. After every test, event, or trial, He honors these deeds and brings delight and satisfaction. Each time I come out of one of these situations, I get stronger. As I stay committed to my health, I continue to grow fiercer in all that I do. I had to teach my children about faith and fear of life. It is my heart's desire for them to be fearless and full of faith. It has been said that fear is false evidence appearing real, and faith is hope manifested, the evidence of things not seen. I know that this experience with my health solidified my faith in God and the power of prayer.

My faith in God has strengthened through fasting and praying, giving me the courage to stay committed to my health. I prayed and trusted God to guide me every step, and He has been faithful to me. I had to rely on God's faithfulness during this season to carry me through. I'm grateful for my faith-filled supporters and family, who kept me covered in prayer. I empower you never to let fear hold you back. Fear did not hold me back because I refused to allow it. I am grateful that God's grace and my faith carried me this far in life. God honored my trust and obedience and delivered me. I'm so grateful to have the gift of faith!

*Knowing my "WHY" was crucial for me:* I believe that knowing your "WHY" in life is another critical part of our journey. I want you to search deep down in your heart and soul for that big *why* in your life - knowing that *why* will guide you through living a purposeful life that is true to your core values. Your *why* is your calling and vision of life, so love what you do and do it because you love it. I had to look deep inside my heart and soul to find my *why* in life.

*~ Featured Author Fa'apepele "Pele" Hunkin ~*

I'm very clear - my children and blessings are my absolute *why* in life. Sure, being a mother is full of challenges, but being a single mom is really difficult. However, overcoming all the battles of being a single mom has been an excellent ride for me. Through many ups and downs, I have dealt with these battles and witnessed them turn into blessings. Rest assured, my *why* was more significant and bigger than what knocked me down. Finding that drive will help you go where you want to go on your path, so I urge you to do so. Remember that you have the strength and bravery to recover from whatever knocked you down. You will quickly understand your purpose once you know your *why* in life.

Knowing your purpose in life will guide you and create an unmistakable path for your life. When doing things from the kindness of your heart with a lot of love brings you joy, you know you are aligned with your purpose. Doing this daily is how I know I am aligned with my God-given purpose. I encourage you to be vessels of love and positivity to fulfill your God-given purpose. I am grateful for all life's challenges that gave me a feeling of appreciation for God's blessings.

*Encountering my challenging obstacles and trials and seeing them as opportunities:* I am grateful for all life's challenges. They actually revealed the goodness of God and gave me a feeling of appreciation for His blessings. I encourage you to be thankful for the pain that strengthened you during the trials of life.

*~ Featured Author Fa'apepele "Pele" Hunkin ~*

Going through life's struggles helped me find my purpose for a meaningful life. I believe my purpose in life is something to be passionate about. I want to positively impact people's lives. I am empowering you to know and understand the importance of living a purposeful life. Rise with the courage to grow through the pain of any situation. Don't just go through the pain of any challenges, trials, tribulations, and tragedies, grow through them too. I really believe that these things are manifested in our lives not just so that we can grow, but also to allow us to see how strong we really are. Honestly, these things don't happen *to* us, they happen *for* us. They are opportunities to improve, be better, and do better.

Therefore, I encourage you not to give up on life when you get knocked down. I want you to know that you are strong enough to live this life. I know my children need me more than ever, so I have to stay strong for them. I am proof of what God can do for you because I didn't quit on life. Quitting was not an option, no matter how overwhelmed I was feeling with my health condition. I would not let a mild atherosclerosis diagnosis take over my life. God created me to be that fierce woman roaring into purpose to make a difference in this world. Therefore, as I walked in this truth, I had to remain grateful with confidence and love. I believe in God, myself, and my unwavering faith in Him, to see me through it all. He can do the same for you - all you have to do is ask Him to come into your life and be willing to trust Him and walk with Him every day.

I allowed my health situation to give me an understanding of what it means to be strong. I am blessed with life because I love myself to do whatever is necessary to live it. Therefore, I will never give up on my hopes and dreams and never give up on me. Remember, you are strong enough to get through any challenge placed in your path. You are a warrior who does not just survive but thrive. Make the most of this one life that you've been given. Live it to the fullest and always have an attitude of gratitude no matter the trials and tribulations of life.

*Learning to love myself and give from my overflow:* In my journey, I Learned to F.L.Y. (First Love Yourself) and to be the change I want to see. I never want to give up being that loving mother to my children, but I can't do that if I'm not healthy and alive. Self-care is not selfish. We have to take care of ourselves so that our loved ones don't have to be burdened with taking care of us. What we do to our bodies and for ourselves matters. Living an unhealthy lifestyle is not fair to our loved ones. The best way to love others is to first love ourselves.

Yes, your love for others is definitely important, but you can't properly love anyone else until you first love yourself. After your love for God and yourself, you should love others. Loving yourself doesn't mean to be arrogant, it means to fill your heart and spirit with enough love to share. I consider myself to be a vessel of love and positivity, meaning that I share my love and spread positivity everywhere I go. Being a vessel of love and positivity in this journey blessed me with the opportunity to inspire, empower, motivate, and educate those who are going through similar situations.

Learn the importance of paying it forward no matter your challenges in life. As the Bible says, it is better to give than to receive. With that in mind, paying it forward is crucial. If someone has poured into you and created an overflow, you must be sure to pay it forward. In other words, be intentional about pouring into others.

My hope is that some part of my story resonated with you and that you gained something from it. I shared it with you because I know how important it is to love yourself. It is a never-ending process, but with God's help, you can certainly do it. I've had the privilege and honor to go through many storms with God by my side. God has allowed so many people to pour into my life and I am compelled to do the same for others. I have no doubts, I owe everything to Him. I will First Love Myself and I will pay the fruits of my labor forward. It is because of Him that I AM MORE THAN A CONQUEROR!!!

*~ Featured Author Fa'apepele "Pele" Hunkin ~*

## *Fa'apepele "Pele" Hunkin*
## *Featured Author*

# About "Pele"

Fa'apepele Hunkin is from the beautiful island of Samoa and is affectionately known as "Pele," which means "Sweetheart" in her native Samoan language.

Pele is a retired United States Army Combat Veteran who served honorably and distinctively for 19 years in various organizations and deployments before retiring as a Sergeant First Class in October 2013. Today, Pele is a dynamic speaker, international best-selling author, six-time co-author, and founder of *Pele Inspire-Embracing Authentic Love*; a widow and devoted mother of four loving children (Nicole, Dean Jr., Victoria, and Isabella).

This fierce woman of God experienced many challenges over her lifetime and credited God for bringing her through many trials and tribulations. She finds strength in sharing the story of her journey with people all over the globe.

She joined the U.S. Army in November 1994 and later married Deanne Ignacio Tajalle, the man she had fallen in love with and the father of her children. Her husband, unfortunately, suffered a fatal accident, which put him in a coma for six months before he finally passed away from the wounds.

Pele is an Ambassador for the *Re-Discover Me* community of Columbia, South Carolina, and *The Women of Dignity Magazine*.

Pele is a University of Management and Technology graduate with a Master's Degree in Health Care Administration (M.H.A.). She is a Life Coach and a certified *Power Voice* global speaker, having been trained to speak by the world-renowned

Global motivational speaker, Les Brown. *Les Brown Power Voice Summit* featured speakers who showcased Pele's apparent oratorical skills.

Pele's divine purpose is to inspire and empower women to know that they are enough so they can be vessels of love and positivity while fulfilling their God-given purpose.

*~ Featured Author Fa'apepele "Pele" Hunkin ~*

# For Such a Time As This

Dr. Angie Gray
Co-Visionary Author

*~ Visionary Author: Dr. Angie Gray ~*

# For Such a Time as This

**By Dr. Angie Gray**

Over the years, I have had the privilege and the honor of hearing countless stories of overcoming and victory. Truth be told, I could also tell countless stories of my own trials and triumphs. It's no secret that life is a series of events and experiences that create our individual stories. Every single one of us has a story to tell. In fact, we have many stories within us; the kind we share and the kind we'd rather take to our grave. I am no different. I grew up in an era of "What happens in this house, stays in this house." I was taught not to air family business. Hence, I've grown up with the idea that my business is my business and there's no reason to share it. I have always been very protective of my family business.

In recent years, however, I've come to believe that our experiences aren't even about us, anyway. Upon closer examination, they are really about being able to develop and share empathy. Empathy seems to be a major missing element from the human experience. Many of us are unable to add to the empathy factor because of our unwillingness to share and expose our vulnerabilities. Instead, we hold on to our stories for dear life, keeping everything inside. The problem with keeping it inside is that there's not enough for everything to stay in place. So, things will begin to slowly, but surely, ooze out. Unfortunately, those things are more often than not, negative. They show up in the hiccups of life as guilt, shame, anger, unforgiveness, promiscuity, addiction, fear, and failure, to name a few. Meanwhile, the empathy, sympathy, love, kindness, patience, forgiveness and the like, all manage to get suppressed and pushed down by the negative.

To add insult to injury, many of us turn to vices hoping to suppress those things that keep seeping out without our permission. Those things that really are pain, hurt, and disappointment, get away from us because they masquerade themselves in negativity and create the wrong energy. Toxic energy causes us to put defense mechanisms and impenetrable walls of insecurity around us. Unfortunately, what's on the outside is most visible. It's much more difficult for people to get a true picture of us because they can only observe what's on the outside. They get this one-sided perspective of us and then they use it to formulate their picture of you. Sadly, without having the benefit of what's on the inside, sometimes that picture is distorted. People start telling us about the image of us that they see and before we know it, we start seeing the same things they see. Before long, we lose sight of who we are. That's when we lose our focus and life becomes blurred.

We all know the horrific side of the Pandemic of 2020 and beyond. I certainly understand that it was not kind in many respects and my heart goes out to everyone who experienced loss of life, loved ones, time, experiences, businesses, opportunities, jobs, etc. Part of the reason that this anthology was titled "More Than a Conqueror" was because many of us managed to survive and conquer insurmountable odds, both pre-pandemic and during the pandemic. The pandemic simply illuminated many of our struggles. Some of them personal and individual and others casting a much wider, global view. While it put tremendous stress and strain on our medical system and the workers that make up the system, the pandemic gave every non-essential worker the opportunity to sit still and reflect. Something that many of may have never actually taken the time to do otherwise. It was like a collective moment of meditation. Of course, these were difficult days and challenging moments that simply built upon each other, day after day, one hour at a time.

The pandemic and the timing of the resulting shutdown of the country coincided with the weekend in which my family had planned to celebrate my birthday. I was so excited because we were going to see a play and go out for dinner. I absolutely love spending time with family, making memories, and having fun. I'm a staunch believer in the importance of celebrating and think we should all be very intentional about it - whether the occasion is big or small.

As with any crisis, some found this to be an opportunity. The crisis was so huge and overwhelming that the impact roars on, even today. That saying many of us have heard, "We're not out of the woods yet," certainly rings true in this case, even though it's been over two years since it first began. I've faced many trials and tribulations in my life. My mother and my grandmother often reminded me to look at any situation, no matter how bad it seemed, to find the good in it. I still try to do just that. The shutdown was no different for me. I spent a lot of time talking with others and listening as they told me of the situations they were experiencing amidst the crisis. In looking for the good in the situation and helping them to reframe it to focus on the positive elements, I offered words of hope and inspiration, but more importantly, I tried to get them to see the beauty beneath the ashes. I eventually would come to coin the phrase, "The crisis was the opportunity you never knew you needed."

As a woman of God, two things I know for sure is that you will face many trials and tribulations and secondly that God will use those things to grow you and show you. By that I mean, God allows these situations and circumstances so that we can grow through them and learn the valuable lessons they offer. Taking it a step further, these things also give us the opportunity to see God's hand at work and to grow our faith. I firmly believe that our experiences mold and shape us and that every one of them offer two things; a lesson and a blessing. We build our perspectives upon these experiences and create how we view our life and the world at-large. We've all heard the adage that some view the glass as half-full and others view it as half-empty. I want to encourage you to look through the "half-full" lens. This is the approach I took during the shutdown.

The shutdown/crisis afforded us the opportunity to slow down. I felt like it gave me a chance to get off the *merry-go-round of life*. Like so many, I actually took time out to reassess my life and some of the trials and tribulations that I've gone through. Much to my surprise, I came to realize that I didn't just *go through* those things, I actually did *grow through* them. Some of the pain, hurt, and disappointment that I went through knocked me off my feet and took my breath away. I got the wind knocked out of me and got knocked to my knees. At the time, I had no idea that these things that were happening *to* me were actually happening *for* me. I say that because I was devastated and had no words for how I felt. I felt like I was all alone and that no one could possibly understand what I was going through. Those very events and feelings led me to prayer and reflection, and they certainly brought me closer to God.

Of course, now that I've made through some of these storms, I know just how resilient I am and that there is refuge in God. We all have heard, "This too shall pass," and of course, it will, but that doesn't make it feel any better when you're going through it. People face incredible pain points throughout their life and sometimes they get stuck in those very moments and can't seem to get out. Those are the people for whom this book is written. The authors are pouring out from the depths of their soul, not because they want to re-live these moments of excruciating pain or they just want to play "one-upmanship." So often, we experience circumstances that have the power to change who we are, how we think, and how we approach life and our relationships. These life changing moments are powerful because they can define us and the rest of our life.

I know from personal experience, some things hurt us to our very core and crush our Spirit. In the words of the character, Donkey in the movie Shrek, "You cut me real deep just now!" Trust me, I've been there and I can definitely relate. It doesn't feel good. It's not just disappointing, it's painful. In fact, it hurts like hell. The things I'm talking about are certainly not fun or easy. I'm talking about divorce, sexual assault, miscarriage, bankruptcy, loss of loved ones, witnessing up close and personal alcoholism and addiction, domestic violence, infidelity, promiscuity, public persecution, and so much more. The wisdom I want to leave with you is that you can use these pain points for good. God's word assures us that those things meant for our harm will be used for our good. There's so much truth in that.

I want you to know that some of our greatest moments of pain fuel our passion. The passion I'm speaking of is, at its essence, righteous indignation. It's the kind of anger that gets caught in our hearts and mind. The kind of anger that gets stuck in your throat and you just can't shake it. You go to sleep thinking about it and you wake up thinking about it. You think about it throughout the day. It's that prolonged anger that no matter how hard you try to let it go, you just can't. The pull of righteous indignation is so strong that it's mentioned multiple times in the bible. This righteous indignation fuels passion, and passion ignites purpose.

You have options when dealing with your pain. You can try to ignore it, do nothing, and allow it to fester and infect you. I think a better option is to actually deal with it and treat it so that the healing can begin before it has time to seep into your bloodstream. I like to say that you have to revisit your P.A.S.T. because that's the most logical starting point. That's where you first noticed the pain point that you can't shake. Think of the PAST as "Purpose Always Starts There." I don't want you to dwell in the past, but I do want you to revisit it for the purpose of reflection and uncovering your purpose. I actually believe that your greatest pain will lead you to your greater purpose.

Yes, we've all been through some things that could've defined us, but I believe they were just defining moments that were shaping us into the image we were designed to be. So, I call them designing moments rather than defining moments.

These very moments could have defined who we were, but let's allow them to design who we will become. Reflect just long enough to get some clarity about who you want to become and how you can use what you've gone through to help you get there. There's no need to get stuck there. My best advice is; go back, pick up what you need, leave what you don't need, and then move forward and go toward where you need to get to.

You see, I don't consider these designing moments to be a bad thing. In fact, I think they are actually good for you. No doubt they hurt, but as you've likely heard, what doesn't kill you strengthens you. Without these designing moments, you can't be in the position of power that experience puts you in. Your power lies in the fact that you can rely on what you know rather than what you've read about or heard about. Use that power for two things; one to grow your faith and two to show His faith.

Don't tell your business - share your story. There is a difference! Telling your business just creates busyness, but sharing your story promotes hope and healing. Use your story to improve and evolve yourself, but more importantly, to encourage and support somebody who is lost and trying to turn their defining moment into a designing moment. You can be the change and the sign they were looking for. It's so easy to find ourselves in situations that make us feel like giving up. I'm going to keep it real - it is so much easier to give up and throw in the towel. Fighting and conquering require a lot more effort, but the result is so much better. I want you to understand that when you fight - you win, but when you give up - you lose. You've heard this before: "Quitters never win and winners never quit." This is a genuine statement that we can use as a reminder to hang in there and never give up - you are More Than a Conqueror!

You have been built to handle any adversity thrown at you. From the moment we are conceived, we are given some unique things: gifts, talents, purpose, plans, DNA and fingerprints, to name a few. Your Creator has sewn these unique qualities within you for many reasons, but the greatest of these is so that you can help build His kingdom. This is why He will support you in everything you do to advance the kingdom. That's why when bad things happen to you, He will turn them around and use them for your good. It's not even really about you, per se. Really, it's about the fact that we are all connected and when one of us rises, we all rise. Part of the pandemic was to show us this truth.

The things you've gone through - no matter how devastating or ugly - have built your strength and your character. Your character is who you are when no one is looking. People can take away your things, but no one can take away your character. I encourage you to work every day to improve your character and to hold on to with everything that you are and everything you have within you. Improving your character will ultimately improve the quality of your life. Faith, hope, and love are ingrained in your character. God helps you to develop your character because it is your superpower. Your character houses your integrity, intentions, desires, passion, and divine purpose. This is why God uses your experiences to feed your faith and not your fears. God is not concerned with who you used to be or where you came from; He is solely focused on where you are going and who you are becoming. I can honestly say, I've been through a lot of heartache and despair, but I wouldn't change it. It has prepared me for such a time as this. A time when people all over the world are counting on me for hope, inspiration and motivation. I'm just thankful and grateful to be here for all of it! He is counting on you to use everything you've grown through, **for such a time as this**!

*~ Visionary Author: Dr. Angie Gray ~*

*Dr. Angie Gray*

*Co-Visionary Author*

# *About Angie*

Dr. Angie Gray is a Professional, Personal, and Purpose Development Facilitator who works with people of all ages to empower them to use their God-given purpose, gifts, and talents to become the best version of themselves so they can leave a lasting legacy for the Universe.

Angie strongly believes that we each have a divine purpose in life and that we are much happier and productive when we are walking in that purpose. She is of the strong conviction that when individuals lead a purpose-directed life; the Kingdom is a much better place for everyone. Angie believes that you can design a very intentional blueprint for the life that you yearn to live.

Rev. Dr. Angie Gray is an ordained minister and holds a Doctorate Degree in Religious Studies with an emphasis in Life Coaching & Mentoring, two Master's Degrees: one in Educational Administration and the other in Counseling, and a Bachelor's Degree in Communications and Psychology.

Angie counts it a blessing, honor, and privilege to be a wife and mother of four who also serves on the ministerial team at her church. Angie recognizes and acknowledges that God has anointed and appointed her for every position she holds in life. Using the vehicle, *Empowerment Matters, LLC*, of which she is the co-founder, Angie is here to share her purpose, gifts, and talents to empower all that she encounters.

Dr. Gray is an accomplished public speaker and protégé of internationally renowned motivational speaker Les Brown. Angie also trained with the world-renowned personal development trainer, Brendon Burchard. Angie resides in New Jersey with her family and two dogs.

*~ Visionary Author: Dr. Angie Gray ~*

# Contact Information

# Jodie Solberg

***Psyched Up Success LLC***

**Email**

jodie@psychedupsuccess.com

**Phone Number**

+1-425-608-1867

**Website**

www.psychedupsuccess.com

**Facebook**

https://www.facebook.com/psychedupsuccess

**Twitter**

https://twitter.com/JodieSolberg

**Instagram**

https://www.instagram.com/psyched_up_success

**LinkedIn**

https://www.linkedin.com/in/jsolberg

**YouTube Channel**

https://www.youtube.com/c/JodieSolberg

**Mailing Address**

PO Box 247
Concrete, WA, 98237

*~ Jodie Solberg ~*

# Sonya Howell Barrow

**Email**

sonyahowellbarrow@gmail.com

**Phone Number**

+1-910-729-9130

**Website**

www.sonyahowellbarrow.com

**Facebook**

www.facebook.com/sonyahowellbarrow.biz

www.facebook.com/authorpreneursonya

**Instagram**

www.instagram.com/authorpreneursonya

**LinkedIn**

https://www.linkedin.com/in/sonyahowellbarrow/

# Bernice Johnson

**Instagram**

www.instagram.com/authorbernicejohnson

**LinkedIn**

www.linkedin.com/in/authorbernicejohnson

**Facebook**

https://www.facebook.com/authorbernicejohnson

https://www.facebook.com/BerniceJohnson

**Email**

johnsonbernice829@gmail.com

# Mae Cervantes

Maegnetic Socials

**Email**

maejcervantes@gmail.com

**Phone**

+0-945-448-1487

**Website**

www.maegneticsocials.com

**Facebook**

www.facebook.com/maegneticsocials

**Instagram**

www.instagram.com/maegneticsocials

**LinkedIn**

www.linkedin.com/in/maejcervantes/

**YouTube**

https://www.youtube.com/channel/UC9n5Q2rz6oCSACAA4itmVsQ

**Mailing Address**

Block 2 Lot 3 Victors Executive Homes
Cabantian
Davao City, Davao del Sur 8000

# Coach Teon Singletary

Teon Singletary Leadership Empowerment

**Email**

bless@teonsingletary.com

**Phone Number**

+1-843-344-5181

**Website**

www.TeonSingletary.com

**Facebook**

https://www.facebook.com/teon.singletary

**Twitter**

https://www.twitter.com/TeonSingletary

**Instagram**

https://www.instagram.com/teonsingletary/

**LinkedIn**

http://linkedin.com/in/coachteonsingletary

**YouTube Channel**

https://www.youtube.com/channel/UC8sjsi1_wSV9mYhc0QKvVMQ

**Mailing Address**

85 Broughton Ave
Andrews, SC, 29510

*~ Coach Teon Singletary ~*

# Vanessa Simmons


**Email**

support@vanessa-simmons.com

**Phone**

+1-760-544-3686

**Website**

https://vanessa-simmons.com

**Facebook**

http://facebook.com/vanessasimmons.co

**Instagram**

http://instagram.com/vanessa_simmons

**Mailing Address**

2302 Servando Avenue, Apt. #8
San Diego, CA 92154

# Pele Hunkin


Email

pelehunkin03@gmail.com

Website

www.peleinspire.com

Facebook

www.facebook.com/peleinspire

www.facebook.com/pelehunkin04

Instagram

www.instagram.com/peleinspire

# Connect With Dr. John E. Gray!!!

Dr. John E. Gray

Professor of Positivity

**Email**

drjohn@EmpowermentMattersLLC.com

**Phone**

+1. 856. 442. 9270

**Website**

www.professorofpositivity.com

**Facebook**

@John E Gray

**Twitter**

@drofpositivity

**Instagram**

@professor_of_positivity

**LinkedIn**

@Dr. John E Gray

**YouTube Channel**

https://www.youtube.com/channel/UCdUVk8VOLqqbHTebF58GAYw

**Mailing Address**

Empowerment Matters, LLC
% Dr. John Gray
P.O. Box 84
Sicklerville, NJ 08081

*~ Dr. John E. Gray ~*

DR. JOHN E. GRAY

Dr. John E. Gray

www.professorofpositivity.com

DrJohn@EmpowermentMattersLLC.com

856.442.9270

Here's Another Book by Dr. Gray That You May Enjoy!

## PowerTalk:
Perspectives on Power, Passion, Perseverance, and Purpose
**Volume I and Volume II**

---

Visit his website at

www.professorofpositivity.com

to Get an Autographed Copy!

Here's Another Book by Dr. Gray That You May Enjoy!

## Quitting Was Not an Option: A Journey of Perseverance and Resilience

Visit his website at

www.professorofpositivity.com

to Get an Autographed Copy!

Here's Another Book by Dr. Gray That You May Enjoy!

Above and Beyond:
8 Things Champions Do To Conquer Their Limits

Visit his website at

www.professorofpositivity.com

to Get an Autographed Copy!

# GREAT NEWS!!!!

**There Is A Free E-book that is yours for the asking.**

**Simply send me an email at**

DrJohn@EmpowermentMattersLLC.com

**to request your FREE copy of my E-book *"From Passion to Purpose"***

**Put *"PowerTalk Perspectives"* in the Subject Line**

**AND**

**include a photo of you holding this book**

## *About the Project Manager, Writing Consultant & Content Editor*

**~ Dr. Angie Gray ~**

Having had a love for reading and writing for as long as she can remember, Dr. Angie Gray is truly operating under her umbrella of purpose. Over the years she has won many distinctive awards for her gift of writing. Her accolades go back as far as elementary school when she wrote poetry and traveled throughout her home state of New Jersey to share writing through poetry recitations to churches, associations, and civic organizations.

As the winner of such prestigious awards as the Gannett National Journalism Award and the KYW News Radio Award, Angie's writing skills have served her well. Her writing career has led her to the path of *Bestselling Author* and *International Bestselling Author,* sealing her respect and credentials within the world of writing.

Dr. Gray's degree in Communications and multi-decade career in education has solidified a strong foundation on which to build her project management and publishing ventures to further serve the writing community and the universe-at-large. She attributes her success and achievements to her divine purpose and God-given gifts and talents.

Angie is the co-founder of ***Onyx Expressions,*** LLC and the Amazon Bestselling Author of ***BACK FROM THE BRINK: THE BLESSING OF O NEAR-DEATH EXPERIENCE,*** contributing author of the Amazon International Bestseller, ***THE WOMEN OF THE POWER VOICE*** and the book series, ***ONE GOOD SIP AT A TIME.***

~ *"More Than a Conqueror" Project Manager* ~

## Connect With Our Writing Consultant
## Dr. Angie Gray


Email

drangie@EmpowermentMattersLLC.com

Phone

+1. 856. 270. 8883

Website

www.DrAngieGray.com

Facebook

https://www.facebook.com/DrAngieGray

Twitter

https://twitter.com/DrAngieGray

Instagram

https://www.instagram.com/drangiegray4/

LinkedIn

https://www.linkedin.com/in/dr-angie-gray/

YouTube

https://www.youtube.com/channel/UCEuSQbswnZ-A8CY22FnOKuQ

Mailing Address

Empowerment Matters, LLC
% Dr. Angie Gray
P.O. Box 84
Sicklerville, NJ 08081


*~ "More Than a Conqueror" Project Manager ~*

Thank you for investing your time to read this work. It is straight from our hearts to yours. We truly hope you have found the inspiration, hope, and motivation we put into this effort.

There is definitely an inner author within you waiting to be released. If you are interested in sharing your story with the Universe, reach out to us and we'll help you get started with the process.

~ John & Angie Gray

We know you are **More Than a Conqueror!!**

We also offer project management oversight and consultation for anthologies. **If you need a project manager for your anthology, please reach out to us.** We are here to serve and assist you with creating an amazing anthology of the authors you choose.

ONYX EXPRESSIONS

*~ "More Than a Conqueror" Project Manager ~*

Made in the USA
Columbia, SC
25 January 2024

30831378R00093